My life
is my message.

M.K.Gandhi

ADVANCE PRAISE

This book skillfully pulls together important lessons from diverse exemplars who remind us that to lead effectively, we must be willing to listen, learn, value people and be open to challenging our mindsets so that ultimately we can transform local and global systems for a more sustainable future. To be a true leader, one must stay curious and always be learning.

Dr Mehmood Khan, *Life Biosciences CEO and PepsiCo Former Vice Chairman and Chief Scientific Officer*

Managers manage, leaders lead and inspirational leaders inspire. It's a journey all leaders take, some reach the final stage, but why some and not others? Becoming that leader who inspires means that people follow because they believe in something bigger than themselves, the company that they work for and the product or service that they provide. Fulfillment comes in many forms, but finding it in work can be one of life's greatest pleasures and this book will help many find such fulfillment.

Jeff Hembrock, *Former President, Miller Brewing Company*

Here is an inspirational examination of a wide range of highly effective leaders—of how their individual growth was shaped by determination, focus, courage and life experience. This instructive, thought-provoking analysis has universal and multigenerational appeal to readers at various stages of their career path. It encourages you to be authentic, embrace your uniqueness with pride and dare to reach beyond your comfort zone.

Brenda B. Schoonover, *US Ambassador (Retired)*

In today's hypercompetitive business environment, regardless of industry, culture or geography, defining effective leadership through a lens of bottom line outcomes is misguided and limiting relative to achieving real impact. Blair and Gesner capture what is critically missing by demonstrating the importance of mission-driven leadership, providing a new value proposition in our thinking of what it means to lead inspirationally and intentionally by institutionalizing one's life mission in our work.

Matthew Wagner, PhD, *Vice President of Revitalization Programs, Main Street America, Former SC Johnson Global Community Affairs Director and India Fulbright Specialist*

Humility. Respect. Reflection. These are among the principles critically important for meaningful public service; but how do they inform a person's capacity to be a transformational leader? What this book accomplishes in compelling fashion is to demonstrate that if our leadership isn't grounded in core values that embrace dignity for ourselves and others, then we not only diminish our influence, we diminish humanity as a whole. Lift up yourself, lift up others, read this book.

Thomas Schnaubelt, PhD, *Executive Director and Associate Vice Provost, Haas Center for Public Service, Stanford University*

In an eloquent, yet conversational style, this volume inspires the ordinary to cross over into the extraordinary space of 'power-with' leadership. Interspersing hypothetical conversations of the world's greatest leaders of all time with the narratives of living leaders who inspire, the authors provoke the readers into making impactful meaning from their own lives. The volume spurs us to live to touch lives, to walk the talk and to leave a footprint.

Nalini Bikkina, PhD, *Director-in-Charge, Gandhi Institute of Technology and Management (GITAM) School of Gandhian Studies, and Former Fulbright Academic Excellence Fellow, the University of Nebraska, Omaha*

Achieving the changes our world needs will take leadership. But many of us who care about the common good do not see ourselves as leaders. Blair and Gesner invite us to step back, look at our lives and values, and write ourselves a new story in which we rise to the challenges that matter to us. We have never needed this invitation—and their guidance—more than right now.

Andrew J. Seligsohn, PhD, *President, Campus Compact (USA)*

Young entrepreneurs like the ones we support want their work to contribute to society, but they also want to make enough money to create wealth for themselves and their communities. There's a new generation of leaders like us working to mobilize people, information, resources and capital for the greater good. Applying the lessons in this book can help us achieve the positive influence and impact that we seek.

Que El-Amin, *Co-Founder and CEO, Young Enterprising Society*

A thoughtfully crafted resource for personal and professional growth. The authors nailed it in that being a successful leader begins with leading self, first. This book offers relevant examples and stories from real-world leaders and would be a strong supplement to university leadership courses at all levels. Readers will be invited to reflect on their values and behaviors as a means to be in alignment with their authentic self. The book is a reminder that to be successful, we must stay open to learning and unlearning!

Lisa Gies, Ed.D, Dean, *College of Education and Leadership, Cardinal Stritch University*

Leadership may take different forms around the world, but at its core, transformational leadership is fundamentally the same and can be implemented effectively across geographic regions, disciplines and cultures. Become inspired, as I was, by the insights offered by this diverse mix of industry leaders; examine their common threads and uncover the positive influence that will encourage healthy growth for yourself and the organizations you serve.

Abdulrhman F. Almotery, ME-PD, PhD, *Director of Academic and Training Affairs, Royal Commission Health Services Program, Saudi Arabia*

Go on this inspirational journey to find your best self and the legacy you want to leave behind. Every leader struggles with challenges, and Blair and Gesner provide practical, reflective strategies that call upon us to look inside ourselves to deepen our leadership. This is a life-changing must-read for anyone looking to find their sense of purpose and particularly valuable for those aspiring to create educational systems that will inspire a new generation of mission-driven teachers and students.

Dr Courtney Orzel, *Superintendent of Schools, Lemont SD113A, Lemont, Illinois*

Delivered at just the right time, this book inspires leaders to move intentionally towards the clarity of mission-driven lives. Nancy Stanford Blair has generously shared her expertise guiding several generations of leaders in occupational therapy as a part of the AOTA Leadership Development Programs. Together, Blair and Gesner extend the wisdom of 100+ leaders across business, education, health care, non-profits and military who are successfully engaged in building sustainable leadership. Give yourself the gift of time to read this book and enrich your own leadership development.

Ginny Stoffel, PhD, *American Occupational Therapy Association (Ex-President)*

YOUR LIFE IS YOUR MESSAGE

YOUR LIFE IS YOUR MESSAGE

Discovering the Core of
Transformational Leadership

NANCY STANFORD BLAIR
MARK L. GESNER

ATLANTIC
PUBLISHERS & DISTRIBUTORS (P) LTD

ATLANTIC
PUBLISHERS & DISTRIBUTORS (P) LTD
7/22, Ansari Road, Darya Ganj, New Delhi
Tel.: +91-11-4077 5252, 2327 3880
E-mail: orders@atlanticbooks.com
Web: www.atlanticbooks.com

Published by Atlantic Publishers & Distributors (P) Ltd 2024

Previously Published by SAGE Publications in 2019

Printed & bound in India by Atlantic Print Services

DEDICATION

To the transformational leaders of the future,
especially Sarah, Rowan, Anastasia, Adelaide,
Rocco, Ever, Eero and Jude

CONTENTS

FOREWORD

Shortly after my first book, *It's Not about the Coffee,* was published, I was asked to share the book's message of servant leadership with a unique doctoral program in Milwaukee, Wisconsin. I was surprised to find a large group of eager doctoral students engaged in a deep conversation about values-based leadership. The doctoral program at Cardinal Stritch University is based on the Franciscan values of compassion, caring and putting others first. What a winning combination for learning about leadership!

It was there that I met the co-founder of the program and a senior professor, Dr Blair. Nancy asked to interview me for a research project on leaders who serve. Our talk together ranged from our shared interest in servant leadership to the belief that leadership capacity can be, and should be, developed in others, especially those who we might otherwise overlook. We discovered a shared passion for the development of future leaders and supporting those already tasked with the role.

Now, years later, I am delighted to know that the ideas Nancy and I shared helped contribute to the valuable guide about transformational leadership that you are about to read. Nancy and her co-author, Mark Gesner (who was one of the doctoral students mentioned earlier and a leader in his own right), have come up with an engaging and practical approach to help both current and future leaders take a hard look at who they are, and why they want to lead. It's a good read that gives you an opportunity to realize your own leadership possibilities, and the possibilities you and others have to effectively serve and positively transform your businesses, organizations and communities.

It's interesting to see all of the characters in this book (including me), who help make the point that leadership isn't about a title or office, it's about who you are, why and how you do things and what you aim to accomplish. In my own life, I've had experience with a cast of characters not always as insightful as the ones in this book. From when I sold furniture in small family-owned furniture store in Oregon to when I tried to open up coffee shops in Japan, I learned that to be successful I had to put people first, stop thinking that I had all the answers and really listen to the people closest to the business. I also learned that I'm not perfect (and no one else is either), and that sometimes you have to fail to move forward.

Nancy and Mark have given you the luxury of being able to meet a lot of insightful people who've had great accomplishments like transforming large companies, combating poverty and building small businesses and community organizations. Listen to these folks, put aside the fancy titles and see how they made their dreams into realities. They won't (and shouldn't) stop you from making your own mistakes, but they will give you a far better shot of recognizing wisdom when you see it, and appreciating and developing authentic leadership within yourself and those you serve.

Similar to *It's Not about the Coffee*, and my second book, *The Magic Cup*, *Your Life Is Your Message* is about digging deep to find your own core values, aligning those values to your core purpose in life and, as the authors say, 'letting your life SPEAK for itself'. As a businessman, I believe this book highlights the kind of leadership that can ultimately make for the happiest customers, whether they be your employees, shareholders, consumers or, most importantly, you and those you love. This book is also an invitation to listen to yourself and others, live your life with passion and focus on what matters most. These are the sorts of things that I believe make a real difference in work and in life—but what all too many people fail to understand or choose not to act upon. A failure to act on what you know to be true is just a road to nowhere—a path that's easy to take, but won't ever make your dreams come true.

Some may be skeptical about the power of values-based leadership and putting others first, but I can speak first-hand that it makes all the difference in the world. I spent 21 years growing Starbucks into a worldwide phenomenon, growing the company from 25 stores to 15,000 worldwide. Take it from me, this works! As a matter of fact, I believe it's the only type of leadership that is reliable, sustainable and yields the long-term return on investment that meets all the right dashboard indicators, both personal and professional.

As I like to say, 'only the truth sounds like the truth'. This book offers you the chance to discover your truth, see if you like what you hear, and then shape it into the influence and positive outcomes you want to see and be in the world. My advice to you is to say 'yes' to this opportunity, get to know yourself and unleash the powerfully aligned leader within. You might even enjoy reading it over a good cup of coffee.

Enjoy the journey!

Howard Behar
Retired President, Starbucks Coffee Company,
North America and Starbucks Coffee International;
Author, Speaker, Advisor

ACKNOWLEDGEMENTS

They say it takes a village to raise a child. We say it takes a community of support to create a book such as ours. We are so grateful to all those who have sustained us throughout this journey, knowing full well that *Your Life is Your Message* would not have been possible without them. Our appreciation goes out to our many supporters and in particular to:

Our thousands of students and seminar participants through the years. Thank you for inspiring us to write this book in the first place. You are the reason we sought to reach a wider audience and have been the genesis of so many of our ideas.

Our early readers and advisors, Gregg and Bridget Dougherty-Herman, Esther Letven, Pat and Jim Magestro, Donna Recht, David Weitzman and Claire Schneider. Thank you for your early, honest and supportive feedback that set us on the right path and gave us the confidence to continue.

Our guide and mentor in India, Prasad Gollanapalli. Thank you for welcoming us into the heart and soul of your beautiful country and for connecting us to so many amazing servant leaders. Our visits have been spectacular and impactful because of you.

Our colleagues and advocates, Dr Arun Pandey and Priyam Pandey for helping us to make initial publishing connections that helped us move our manuscript forward. We were so very fortunate to have the benefit of your intellect, kindness and contacts. You led us to a spectacular team ably led by Manisha Mathews. Her guidance, responsiveness and professionalism have turned our vision into a reality.

Our generous interviewee, Howard Behar, thank you for not only sharing your transformational leadership story but also for graciously offering to provide the Foreword of this book.

Our loving, patient and supportive families who have wondered when we would ever be done! Deep and sincere thanks to Ron, Alix and Nick, and to Margaret and Sarah. Thanks also to Zick and Meri-Jane for your gentle critiques and publishing acumen.

Finally, good reader, we want to acknowledge you for your bravery. Picking up this book took some curiosity, but reading it through and completing the work within will take courage. We will be forever grateful that you can now be added to the ranks of transformational leaders making our world a better place.

A special acknowledgement to our illustrator, Nick Blair. Thank you for listening, visioning and creating the images that conveyed our thoughts. Your partnership, responsiveness and talent are so very much appreciated.

A NOTE ON NICK BLAIR

As an industrial designer, Nick Blair specializes in obtaining a deep understanding of how people relate to their products, culture and each other. He strives to uncover unmet needs and deploy dynamic product and service solutions to fulfill a meaningful purpose.

PREFACE

Just Before You Enter

This book is a guide. Not only written for the businessperson interested in understanding the world in terms of both mission and margin, but also for the struggling-yet-determined college student, for the teacher or school leader trying to make sense of increasingly complex educational systems and for the parent trying to remain mindful of what else there is to accomplish beyond getting the daily chores completed. This book is also for the person who is simply seeking to survive—putting forth every ounce of energy to overcome daily internal or external struggles and fighting for a future that is brighter than today. This book is about leadership, not as a position or title but as a matter of influence—the type of influence that serves others, organizations and communities near and far. In sum, this book is for all people wanting to find the leader within and who seek to expand their influence over themselves, others and the world in which they live and work.

More pragmatically, this is a book that draws upon lessons learned from interviews with leaders around the world. By reading the forthcoming pages, you will glean insights from interviews with famous people who have run large businesses and governments, and from people not so famous who have led schools, non-profit organizations and communities. You will also read and benefit from our lived experience of teaching and learning with thousands of 'ordinary' people, almost all of whom seem to share a common excitement when they find the path in which their values and actions align to yield the results they envisioned.

We have considered the insights from the leaders interviewed, along with the experiences of our students and colleagues, in the context of what has been written in theories about identity and personal transformation. We have woven together these threads into a unifying model to guide individuals forward through the very personal journey they hope to take. It's this distinct journey that provides a framework for this book and a roadmap for people exploring their ways of being, seeing and doing. It's a book that we believe has broad implications for how to nurture the good in each of us—in each of you—so that we all in turn can nurture the common good. And it's a book that we think is most powerfully viewed and interpreted through each individual's very personal lens.

The title of this book is borrowed from Mahatma Gandhi's words and honors the profound way in which he approached the world. When he was asked by a reporter to sum up his life's work, he responded simply, 'My life is my message.' We are similarly offering the opportunity to take stock of your lives and discover your core message, purpose and desired impact. We can all benefit from the reflective journey of self-examination about the compelling questions of life: Who am I? Why am I here? What do I want to accomplish? How will I go about it? The answers to these questions form the core of transformational leadership, the ability to elevate the self so that you in turn can create positive change by inspiring and influencing meaningful growth within others.

The purpose of this book is to enable all of us to live a powerfully aligned existence where our life becomes our message—a message filled with hope and positive results. This journey represents nothing less than a time for a transformational shift in the way we progress forward and the results we achieve.

Along with striving to be responsive to the general sense of wanting more in life that many people we have met seem to yearn for, our goals for this book are quite specific. Our intent is that you will:

1. Realize that you have the capacity to lead with positive influence in relationship to your colleagues, family, friends and fellow citizens, realizing furthermore that the world desperately needs your leadership now.
2. Develop a growth mindset about yourself and how to be engaged, inspired and tenacious in pursuit of your continued evolution.
3. Recognize the path you are on and gain clarity about how to move forward on that path to realize the goals and outcomes you seek.
4. Increase knowledge and expand your capacity to reach your professional and personal goals by utilizing practical tools

and strategies that increase your effectiveness as a leader, enable you to become a more present and engaged community member and, ultimately, yield an overall stronger you.

5. Understand and appreciate how your transformation as an individual leads to empowering not only your business or organization but the greater good.

The principal tenet within these goals is that interconnectedness exists throughout all we do and hope to achieve. In the end, by elevating the self we elevate others and the systems in which we reside. Ironically, we must be selfish by first bolstering our personal strength and fortitude, so that ultimately we can be selfless in contributing the positive energy and wisdom that our families, businesses, organizations and world need to survive and thrive.

In the pages ahead, you are first met with a series of invitations that give a glimpse of what's to come and that are designed to entice you to boldly enter into the adventure ahead. You are then provided with an initial orientation to this book and our central model of the ascending spiral of transformational leadership, a framework that guides your progression upwards as you learn to discover and clarify the following:

1. Your **who—**the personal exploration of values and the formation of your singular identity
2. Your **why—**the mission and purpose that drive and inform all that you do
3. Your **what—**the identification of the outcomes and goals you seek
4. Your **how—**the tools for the ways in which to realize those goals

After learning about the foundational principles that frame this book, your journey will follow the path of Joseph Campbell's monomyth of the hero's journey. A journey that begins with getting ready for the quest, then enters into the heart of the adventure of gaining clarity and self-empowerment, and concludes with gaining strength and sustenance for the return to daily life. A journey that ultimately creates a transformative shift to a more satisfying and aligned way of being and leading in the world.

Part I of the book starts with you getting introduced to composite profiles of fellow travellers who represent varied levels of personal development and awareness. We think it's important that you take the time to get to know these characters as they serve as reference points for the multiple lenses and stages of development all of us can encounter. Once you have taken the time to understand the stories of others and consider your own, you are challenged to accept the invitation that suits you best, and then proceed forward to prepare for your own transformational leadership discovery process. Before you fully immerse yourself in the journey, Part I also tests your resolve with a contextual reference about why the world needs your leadership now more than ever. The opening section concludes with a primer about how to be fully present and engaged as you progress forward.

In Part II of the book, you are given the opportunity to cross over the threshold to begin your journey in earnest. Your first steps into new territory are aided by a luminary group of transformative and servant leaders who consider their own early forays into transformational thinking, being and doing. Together with Mahatma Gandhi, Dr Martin Luther King, Jr., St. Francis of Assisi, Mother Teresa and the Prophet Muhammad, you are challenged to consider what influenced your own formation and identity. Following the lessons of these nobles, the next four chapters thrust you deeply into and through the ascending spiral of our transformational leadership model. You will learn to wrestle with and clarify your *who*, articulate your *why*, know your *what* and determine your *how*. Throughout Part II, you will meet many of the extraordinary leaders interviewed, all of whom have wrestled with these compelling questions and have learned to successfully integrate the lessons learned into their lives and leadership.

In Part III of the book, you will take on perhaps the greatest challenge of all by actually starting to live your new-found path and gather the tools and wherewithal that you need to move forward with clarity and resolve. You will gain greater appreciation of the depth of the transformational change in which you are engaged and will learn about and adapt four necessary dimensions for sustainability. And finally, as your journey comes to a close, you will discover that the core to your transformation lies within and is a place where you feel completely at home.

Throughout the book, there are stories of our interviewees, illustrations, theories, models and practical examples offered to bring depth, meaning and relevance to the ideas being shared. Learning expeditions are included so that you can reflect upon and practice what you are reading about and more substantively connect with the perspectives being offered. While there are certainly many resources and inspirational stories about others integrated throughout the book, there is also this fundamental truth: the story that should take precedence and the one that matters most is your own. Use all the devices, all of the inspiring exemplars and all the references in ways that speak to your sensibilities.

This book first helps you to prepare for the journey, immerse yourself in transformational thoughts and explorations, and then finally return to your daily life, equipped with a clear path, disposition and set of tools that you need to progress forward. It's a progression that will enable you to gain the necessary clarity to not only know your message but to also speak your message with aligned words and actions influencing the type of change you want to see in your daily life and in the world.

Now, just before you pack your bags and get ready to go, this cautionary note is in order: the road to transformation, empowerment and effective leadership can be rocky and unsettling. If you're truly open to new possibilities, sometimes the path will be painful, comical and even disorienting. As a result, you will be tempted to retreat back to what you're used to—your normal way of doing things that may be adequate but not exceptional. We hope you won't settle for that path—we think if you wanted to settle, you wouldn't be reading this book.

Now we challenge you to think about your life's message—is it the message you desire? Do you feel comfortable in your own skin and are you living your life to its fullest? Only you can be the judge. As the authors, we feel compelled to wake you up—just as this process has awakened us. Further, as Lord Alfred Tennyson suggested, we want to urge you to 'drink life to the lees' by discovering the path that is most compelling and empowering for you.

INVITATIONS

About What Entices Us and Influences Our Direction

There are three invitations in the following pages. In all likelihood, one in particular will resonate with you. You will read an invitation that fits well enough into your story that makes you want to invest and persevere. As you find the invitation that truly works for you, the one that poses opportunities in a way that you find compelling, consider what enticed you. Did you need to be cajoled, amused, heartened or convinced? What rang true for you and why?

It's worthwhile to notice which invitation works for you because it's probably the one that gives you the confidence to move forward with clarity and conviction. It's the one that has value in your eyes. It's the one that empowers you to respond to what Joseph Campbell once named 'the call to adventure' in his description of the hero's journey (Campbell, 2008). Since you are the hero of this story, find the invitation that breaks you free from the pull of inertia. Discover the one that calls your name and suggests a pathway forward that will foster your growth and development. It's a big deal to accept this invitation, so choose wisely. It's your decision as to how you will proceed; own your choice. Know you chose to accept or not to accept an invitation with good reason. Resist stagnation. Make purposeful progress. Open your invitation.

AN INVITATION

FOR THE WANDERERS

What do you need right now?
What will satisfy your thirst?
Do you know?

Who are you?
What's your reason for being?
Do you want to risk finding the answer?

Why do you care?
Can you identify what values guide your path?
Do you have a mission you're bold enough to assert?

What is the impact you hope to achieve?
Do you have influence that makes you proud?
What will be the result of your journey?

How will you navigate your path?
Who and what will guide you?
Are the steps you're taking in the right direction for you?

This is your invitation to enter and explore
To meet others, real and imagined, who are on the journey
If you're tempted by transformation, come in
If you're overwhelmed or underwhelmed, come in
If you're frightened by your complacency, come in
If you have tasted fulfillment and know it's in reach, come in
If you want to serve others and feel alive, come in

You have made it to the doorstep
It appears you are in the right place
A place not only intoxicating because of its potential
A place intoxicating because it is real, powerful and exciting
A place and path where you will have the opportunity
To understand who, why, what and how...
Your life is your message

AN INVITATION

FOR THE DUBIOUS

Please consider joining the conversation
Meet people from around the world and in your neighborhood
Who have transformed organizations and communities
Who have elevated themselves, others and systems

Think pragmatically about your work and life
And if you might be intrigued to challenge your sensibilities
To allow for some personal and professional growth
To leverage your assets and overcome your deficits

Think about your kid, your colleague, your neighbor
Think about your legacy
Consider setting aside your scepticism
Try listening and looking through the lens of others
Think about venturing beyond the mundane, beyond every day

This is your invitation to assess the possibilities
To observe and perhaps understand
How leaders make sense of the world and lift it up
This is your invitation to tweak or even transform
Your own capacity...your own ability...your own priorities

If you decide to enter:
You will learn about theory and practice
You will be encouraged to question your assumptions
You will not be coerced or fooled
But you will see how others have excelled
And you will decide how to apply those lessons to yourself

If you must know how the story ends
Leave now
If certainty and linear progression are necessities
Move along
If you desire absolutes
Absolutely go about your business

Yet if the reason you opened this invitation
Still intrigues you
If you think there might just be more potential and possibility
More ways to contribute, empower and find value
Accept

AN INVITATION

FOR THE COMMITTED

The time has come
To dream, wake up and engage
To be alive and present
To seek, explore and discover

You are ready
To follow your path and make sense of your journey
To set aside any remaining pessimism or hesitation
To examine the landscape and discern the way forward

You can adapt and respond
To the fear of discomfort
To cross the threshold
And to navigate the rough terrain
It's a course you don't always want but dearly need

You're eager for this adventure
Because it's where
You are able to serve, lead and feel fulfilled.
It's a chance to accelerate your evolution and help build the greater good
A route that connects to your core and
Develops your brain, expands your heart and feeds your soul

This is your invitation to
Let go of your acceptance of the ordinary
Hold on to your values and sense of justice
Let in a way of existing that's way beyond today
A place to believe and belong

In this place, you will ask questions
To understand your who, why, what and how
You will take risks and seize opportunities but do no harm
You will venture way beyond today
You will learn your way home

Come explore
Come soar
Come thrive
Come experience
Come in, come in

ON YOUR WAY

While you're thinking about your response to the invitation that suits you best, and before you answer, read on for a more complete orientation to the book and an opportunity to examine your own life story. And then, before you decide whether to take a deeper dive towards your core, determine how and why (or even if) you are choosing to RSVP and accept the invitation.

ORIENTATION

She who has a who, knows no bounds

—The authors

All of us at some point share that common desire to strive for more. More purpose, more fulfillment, more success, more connection, more ability to realize our greatest potential. And to realize your greatest potential, no matter what your initial vantage point may be, it's essential to start with *who*.

Starting with *who* is the linchpin of this book. It's the origin of our model about how great leaders function effectively and, it's what our research suggests, allows people to be comfortable enough with themselves to serve others, transform systems and contribute mightily to whatever cause, business, organization, community or society they wish to impact. Starting with *who* is the ticket that enables you to enter through the opening and progress forward. That is why, in this book, you are challenged to listen and learn from those who have flourished in business, government, education and life so that ultimately you are able to listen to yourself and come to understand the voice where the most profound wisdom surely resides. You are urged to let yourself go so that you can let your self go.

The essential thread of this book, the 'whole' that unifies the variety of influences and voices that appear on the pages ahead, is the model that you see on the following page. It's a model that captures the journey of many of the greatest transformational leaders in the world. It's a model that offers you a path forward from your current state of being, which may at times feel scattered or unfocused, to a place of more purposeful existence and action. It's a roadmap of how to proceed forward to accomplish your greatest ambitions while at the same time be responsive to the people, ideas and causes that you hold dear.

The model starts with the concept of *who* and encourages a deep dive into understanding your core values and what you believe to be your essential truths. The journey then continues to explore your *why*, a gentle but certain push for you to discover your mission in life for yourself and with others. Once you know your *who* and *why*, then the adventure becomes more focused on your *what*. *What* is the impact or result you hope to achieve. *What* is the direction you want to head to align your values and actions to a purposeful end point or deliverable. And finally, *how* is the road you need to take to achieve your *what*. Your *how* is comprised of the very sensible tools and strategies you will employ to integrate your *who* and *why* into steps that will yield your *what*. Your *how* is also made up of the attitudes and actions you apply to pursuing your aims, as well as your overarching disposition in facing the world.

We have framed the process of proceeding through the *who, why, what* and *how* as the ascending spiral of transformational leadership shown in Figure O.1. It appears a bit like an inverted tornado. It defines the path for an alternative to command and control leadership and creates a path for elevating your own effectiveness so that you can influence a similar uplifting shift in others.

FIGURE O.1 THE ASCENDING SPIRAL OF TRANSFORMATIONAL LEADERSHIP

Source: Nick Blair

The base of the model is where many of us exist in today's hectic world. A place where there's a maelstrom of emotions, data, opinions and facts swirling around us and at us. It's a whirlwind of activity where it's easy to get lost and overwhelmed. And so, in order to get grounded, we need to get secure about who we are and what we care about. As we move through the spiral, we work towards figuring out our reason for being—our mission for why we work and live with particular priorities and passions. As we ascend further within the tempest, the force becomes more directed and we concentrate on what end result we want to achieve. We get focused. And then finally, we clarify, refine and tighten our approach—the purposeful and practical path by which we will achieve the desired impact for ourselves and the people and systems that matter to us.

To be clear, the process within the spiral is not a linear ascension to some sort of heightened state of nirvana. Rather, it's more of an iterative journey that continuously enables us to gain clarity and coherence as we make sense out of our environs. The ascent is distinguished by our becoming increasingly adept at shaping and directing the force of our collective impact. Our greatest success comes when we learn how to leverage the power of our ascending spiral towards a constructive rather than destructive end point.

If you think about the great leaders of today and throughout history, it's likely they have followed the spiral to its powerful end point. Think about Dr Martin Luther King, Jr. and his unique journey to become the civil rights leader of the 20th century. His *who* was driven by a clear set of core values for equity, fairness and non-violence, fueling a purpose to lead a movement for freedom. His who and why drove the ultimate outcome (his what) of the Civil Rights Act of 1964 in the USA and his how was peaceful, determined and unwavering non-violent protest. Had he lived, his next 'what' would have been the eradication of poverty in the USA. When someone so clear and powerful like Dr King passes, it's more than an individual injustice; it is an injustice to all because his direction was not just self-empowering, it was empowering for all.

Much like Dr King, other visionary leaders in history such as Mahatma Gandhi, Saint Francis of Assisi, Nelson Mandela and Mother Teresa followed the path of the ascending spiral. These nobles, however, were by no means alone in the way they went about their journeys. In fact, many modern-day leaders in business, government and education also followed this same route. As you will learn from reading this book, CEOs like Rich Teerlink of Harley Davidson and Colleen Barrett of Southwest Airlines, civic leaders like the first elected woman Prime Minister of New Zealand, Helen Clark, educators like Michael Barber of England and Kiren, founder of the largest slum school in Ahmedabad, India, all followed a similar trajectory. So can you. Effective leaders, particularly leaders who live a life of service, start with *who*, understand *why*, focus on *what* and proceed with *how*. It is these leaders who enable themselves, others and systems to transcend and realize elevated ways of thinking, doing and being.

The journey up through the spiral can at first be chaotic and demand some extra energy and focus. As things get more coherent, the power involved gets channeled towards more productive results. The experience of moving through the ascending spiral is somewhat similar. At first, you might find yourself trying to grab hold of the concepts and influences that resonate with you, but eventually, if you hold on to what's working for you and let go of the distractions, you'll have an amazing opportunity. You will be able to understand not only the power behind great leaders but, most essentially, the power that drives you to heights you cannot yet imagine, and the purpose that you can begin to sense but not yet fully define.

We know that when a tornado hits the ground it has the power to destroy everything in its path. Powerful winds dislodge buildings, trees and lives, and spit them back out into haphazard, broken pieces of their former selves. We are asking you to consider what happens when you invert that tornado and follow an ascending spiral that elevates and strengthens all that's within its path. Imagine discovering the positive force within the organizations, environments and communities in which you work and live.

More specifically, think about flipping the confusing and sometimes conflicting demands of the people that surround you, and think what it would be like to find your clear purpose and focus within the whirlwind of everyday complexities, mandates and overwhelming expectations. What if you could calmly and powerfully pull the pieces together, have certainty about your direction and realize the fulfillment of influencing and impacting the issues and end products you think are most important? Others have done this repeatedly throughout our world history. So can you.

Whatever realizations you eventually hold onto as a result of reading this book, for now, give yourself the gift of shifting your mindset. Allow yourself to see things from a different vantage point—a new orientation. Enter the ascending spiral knowing there will be some early swirling afoot, and also understanding that if you can navigate the initial rough climate and unsettling winds, your vision can eventually be clear and compelling. Now that you're well situated for the journey, it's time to stop talking about the weather and start doing something about it.

PART I

PREPARING FOR THE JOURNEY

CHAPTER 1

KNOWING YOUR STORY AND INTENT

About the Stories We Tell through the Lenses We Wear

It seems to be a universal truth that we can appreciate and see things in others that we cannot see or appreciate within ourselves. We can empathize with the struggles someone else faces, and yet have no patience when we can't overcome our own obstacles and inadequacies. When we meet a new person or hear the story about the life of an acquaintance, there's a freedom we give ourselves to acknowledge where that person has been and where he or she is headed. It's just easier to know and appreciate others than to know and appreciate ourselves. And so, to start off on your journey to find our own life's message, it makes perfect sense to first meet some fellow travellers.

In the following pages, you'll be introduced to the stories of Gio, Charlie, Amie, Aarush and Aliyah—a group of people who are at distinctly different stages in their lives. They are fictional characters inspired by very real individuals who we have met along the way.

Each character offers a distinct way of looking at the world while sharing one noticeable thing in common: they are all wondering what will come next in their lives, and they are all wondering if there could be something more. Envision yourself being with each of these individuals on a train or plane, in a hotel coffee shop or hostel common room, and take the time to listen and get to know their stories. We will revisit these individuals throughout the book and refer to their perspectives as ways to understand the leaders interviewed and the principles introduced. It is somewhere amidst the profiles of this cast of characters that you will likely begin to get a clearer glimpse of yourself. Be curious, reserve judgement and make every effort to hear what is being shared—these fellow travellers are speaking to you.

**

GIO: 'I'M FINE'

I'm fine. Completely okay. Really.

Our two-bedroom flat has enough room for a guest and we're near some pretty decent restaurants. We're in a third floor walk-up apartment—which makes me smile. I always tell myself it's got to be a lot like being on the balcony of a fancy Broadway play. You can have a good view of the show and you can also stare at people without them knowing.

Sometimes I stare at people from my balcony just long enough to make up their story. The guy in the suit walks by and I'm sure he can't wait to get home and practice on his karaoke machine to prepare for a Saturday night out with friends who he would like to impress. Then, the much more interesting six foot tall woman walks by smiling. She's thinking about her lover's neck—or the big plate of noodles she's about to eat—or that she just quit her thankless job as an executive assistant—or all three. Then there's the kid about 12 years old. He just stole a candy bar from the corner store and is pleased with himself but scared to go home and face his mother.

Yeah, I like the view from our flat. I also like the commute I have to get to work. I go on the train and I get a kick out of the fact that I can fold the newspaper in one hand, hold the strap handle in the other hand and read about three articles during the ride without losing my balance. One column by someone smart, one international news story, then maybe something about a movie star—that's my routine. I'm not sure if all of this is inspiring or ordinary, but it keeps me going to think that I have some redeeming characteristics that perhaps are interesting or mildly amusing. I am proud of the fact that at least I am not addicted to my smartphone.

I think it would be fairly clear to most people that my life is pretty good. My flat has a view, my commute to work is productive and even my relationship feels solid without too much melodrama. I don't think I'm any sort of elitist. Actually, I seem to blend right in with the masses, maybe because of my olive skin, maybe because I know what clothes fit me, maybe because I don't overstep my bounds.

But here's the thing, I feel like too often I'm driven by inertia and that's when I get scared. Sometimes as a way of coping, I even start to go a bit numb. The numbness helps protect me against getting hurt, against being overwhelmed with any sort of critique of my superficiality and against being underwhelmed with my own mediocrity. The numbness also works as a way of driving away the demons whispering in my ear—telling me that I'll piss away my life watching people from the balcony, making up stories that aren't real, going back and forth and back and forth in a life that is fine... okay... steady—an observer with no influence.

Fortunately, I think, I have learned a little about how to chase away the demons and wake up and get my head and heart connected to something of actual significance. I have two main strategies. First, I think back to the people in my life who supported me, or who at least cared enough to spend time listening to me. There was my grade school teacher who was so impressed with my joke telling that she paraded me around the school to tell a joke to every teacher in the building. There was my friend at work who had non-stop curiosity and kept asking me questions about every imaginable aspect of what I thought and felt. Eventually, I learned to finish my answer with a question to get a rest from his interrogation. There was also my friend, the storyteller, he had a photographic memory and could recount verbatim a passage from a book, or he could just as easily tell me a parable about a river. It didn't matter much, he was always thinking and imagining, and he always had time for me. These teachers and friends of mine, they helped me feel like I mattered—like I was worth the effort. When I get numb or even a little disheartened, I think about their lessons and their connection. And then for the most part I get back on track.

My second strategy is to interrupt my daily life and go traveling. I know lots of people never get this privilege—and I'm thankful for it. Out in the world, away from my balcony, it's where I really come alive. I look out and appreciate the amazing sight of a mountain, a marketplace or a sunrise over the water and I begin to wake up. I go to the kind of places that I could only read about as a kid. Back then, the other kids on my block thought it was a big deal to walk uptown and watch the expensive cars drive by. I didn't get so excited by that stuff—although I did wonder about what the people driving those cars did during the rest of their lives.

I tune in most when I meet people in foreign lands. I step down from the balcony, get out of my own head, and I just am. I start learning directly from people like the tea taster in Darjeeling who knows the distinctions between German, Japanese, Russian and American tastes. I get absorbed in the words of the poet in El Salvador, who doesn't judge me because of my government's ugly past of destroying his people, but rather he explains to me his understanding about how a government and its people don't always agree. And I relish the perspective of the humble doctor in Dubai who helps me appreciate why it's important to serve only three sips of Arabian coffee so that she can continue to have the honor of serving her guests again and again.

The wisdom of people I meet while traveling helps me get beyond my daily frames of reference. It's not only that they provide kernels of truth or examples of goodness—they know how to engage. Maybe it's actually a combination of factors. When I am on the road away from home, I don't care so much about appearances. I want to listen and learn, and I don't need to prove anything. As a result, I wake up, I smile more and I think and feel more deeply. I'm present.

These two strategies—of calling upon past mentors who help me feel like I matter, and escaping into travel encounters that help me feel present—shake me up in a compelling way and remind me that my life is worth living. I become a believer in the importance of engaging in this world, and I feel like I belong rather than just being a passing voyeur. I believe in the possibilities. My mother once told me that she knew I'd be an explorer even before I was born. She said I was always poking around inside her belly. That's why she named me Pelagio, which in Greek means something like 'excellent sailor'. My friends call me Gio, which works for me because it makes me a little different. Being unique, checking out new places—it's all good—I don't want to be ordinary.

The trouble comes when I feel the numbness and no one really notices. I almost don't notice myself. In my head I shut people out, but they don't seem to care. I look from the balcony but can't come up with a story. I ride on the train and instead of being glad to blend in, I feel like I'm not really there. I go back and forth to work and say that I'm fine, but I'm not connecting with anyone. My perspective changes. I'm not doing anything of value. I can't sustain curiosity—only old habits and inertia.

Maybe you think all of this is crap from someone who is self-absorbed and needs the occasional wake-up call to not be completely disgusting. Well, I don't really care because here's the reality: I can't figure out my next step. If my mother was still alive, I'd tell her I'm lost at sea. I'm stuck in a whirlwind of activity that is getting harder and harder to break—a cycle that's controlling me rather than me controlling it. All too often I don't know who I am or where I stand. I don't know why I can't maintain balance anywhere or move forward towards a clear destination—except when I'm in the train, and that's not enough. Really, it's not enough for a human being.

I want to impact others like the teacher, the tea taster and the poet. I want to turn parts of my life upside down, and I'm losing patience with myself—and my little jump-start strategies don't sustain me for any significant length of time. In fact, they're becoming less effective—bordering on pathetic grasps at an elusive existence.

There's more for me, surely there is. I don't want to be fine. I don't want to be okay. I want to get over myself and find a way of being that's as far away from numb as possible. Feeding off others rather than depending on my own core seems temporary at best and selfish at worst. Holding a newspaper on a train just can't be my proudest moment.

★★

CHARLIE: 'KNOW WHAT THEY WANT'

It all boils down to knowing what people want. It's the secret to business, relationships and even self-fulfillment. Seriously, it's true.

Take me, for example. The people who make me happiest know my tastes, my style and what I look for in a good deal. The French chef at my favourite restaurant knows that I like my carrots the size of my pinky and not my forefinger. And of course he knows not to overcook the carrots—not only would that be bad form but he understands that I don't want my vegetables to be mush so he makes sure they have just the right texture—just the right crunch.

The street vendor who I buy my coffee from each day also has my interests in mind. I like cream and sugar, but not too much of either. I want to taste that distinct, strong coffee bean, but just temper it a little bit, give it the comfort of smooth dairy goodness, mixed with a touch of sweetness.

In relationships, all I need is variety, spontaneity and some good attention. Most of my friends are interesting in one way or another, and they're there when I need them. In return, I try to provide my friends with what they want. Arron periodically wants to rant about politics, have me argue with him and then eventually agree with his fundamental point that all politicians are corrupt or inept. No harm there. Josephine likes to point out the quirks in people and how those quirks make life more interesting. So I talk politics with Arron and tell Josephine when I've met someone intriguing. They're pleased, and so am I.

Before I explain how all of this fits into business and has yielded me the success that I now have, let me be clear that it's not just knowing what others like, but knowing what you like for yourself. For me, it's not just well prepared carrots and coffee, it's making my way through the day with cleverness and confidence.

For example, to start my day, unlike most men, I shower before I shave rather than the other way around. Too many people think you should shave first so that you can wash off the extra shaving cream in the shower, which makes sense but doesn't help the quality of your shave or the feel of your skin. If you have a hot shower first, then your pores open up, your bristles are softened and the shave is smooth and clean. Knowing the best approach for life's little necessities gives me a kick—a sense of accomplishment for being a step ahead of the other guy. I also get the feeling of being ahead of the game on the days I make my own coffee. I put in the creamer before I pour in the coffee. The result is that it mixes itself and I never have to use a spoon. Pretty clever, eh? I admit it. I like being reminded regularly that I am not average.

As for how to build my confidence, and the sense of confidence others have in themselves, I'll share the secret. Everyone feels better about themselves when things go their way. For me, a good shave, a good coffee, a good meal—they all make me feel like I have my act together and I'm ready for anything.

Learning what people like and responding to those preferences helped me move up from line staff into management quickly at the hospitality business where I used to work, and also now at the management consulting firm where I'm a lead partner. In the hotels, it wasn't only getting the easy stuff right like remembering your customers' names, knowing the way they liked their rooms prepped and having the concierge memorize the best restaurants in town for all different kinds of clientele. That stuff is necessary but not sufficient—everyone needs to know those things or you fail quickly. I knew the subtleties of what makes for a good hotel. Things like dusting the tops of picture frames, sweeping the stairway and polishing the brass doorknobs in plain view of the customers. They need to see you attending to details so that they'll know you will attend to their details. And with the staff, you better know the names of the housekeepers' kids to show that you care and compliment your front desk clerk's haircut. Anybody who combs his hair every hour must appreciate it when you tell him he's well quaffed. Take notice of what people care about, mean what you say whenever possible and people will work hard for you and stay loyal. It goes for customers and it goes for your staff.

And now, the real pay-off—the insight that connects the dots and pulls together the pieces: in work and in life, it's all about relationships and finding rewards for everyone. I haven't read all of those 'art of the deal' books or 'win-win' negotiating techniques. I don't have to because it's all common sense. When you're selling a product or brokering a partnership, you just have to be sure everyone feels like they got what they wanted. At the hotels, for the customers who wanted a little bit of a bargain on their rooms—I gave it to them and they always came back. For the marketing and sales guys who wanted to make sure I'm credible, I'll ask them about their ratios of cold calls versus closures, throw in a few detailed questions about their CRM software and funnels, and then appreciate that they've got expertise that I can't begin to understand. I try not to do this stuff in a fake way, but I always remember, I have to give them what they want—it gives them confidence.

Sometimes I say to myself, 'Charlie, can it all be so easy?' Give people what they want—do it with a little sincerity and the world is a happier, more productive place. Everyone feels like they matter and I feel like I matter. What's not to like? I don't need to meditate to be one with the world. I have my act together.

But then recently, I was at a dinner after finishing a project and my grand plan for success got knocked off course. A business associate who was only loosely connected to the current project, but who had worked with me before, started asking me questions that rubbed me the wrong way. She said she noticed that I seemed pretty pleased with myself, which irritated me because I don't see myself as cocky, just confident. And I never did anything to insult her. She backed up a little and said she didn't mean to offend me, she just really thought I seemed happy with the way my life was going and wanted to ask if that was truly the case. Was I happy and fulfilled?

Usually, questions about fulfillment make me wince. It's not that I don't want fulfillment—hey, I'm all about fulfillment. It's just that when people ask if I'm fulfilled, it's because they think they have some kind of corner on the market of fulfillment and want to see if I've got some deep explanation about my existence. But once

I got beyond thinking this woman was acting superior, I learned that she was pretty sincere. How was I doing? Did I like the path I was on? What really made me interested in life and where was I headed? Did I have what I needed?

Her last question, about what I needed, that's the one that rocked my world. Initially, I told her that I had what I wanted and I meant it. She didn't push back and nodded with a polite smile. I don't think she was judging, just figuring me out. Then she asked again whether I had what I needed. And when I didn't answer, she asked if I knew what I needed. Initially I cringed because I thought she was going to give me a lecture, but she had no lectures, only questions.

Shit. Isn't having all the things I want enough? Isn't being confident and successful enough? Is there some sort of life out there that will provide me with the things I never knew I needed? For me, I know it's not another job. I like my job no matter what anyone says or what sort of psychobabble someone tries to feed me. But this woman, I could see it in her eyes. It was a sense of knowing and being in a place that wasn't just filled with all of the right pieces—it was understanding the whole package. A way of being in which she wasn't only a clever cog but where she felt in sync and in tune—a place that mattered to herself and to others.

I thought—dammit—I matter and I'm having an impact. Good friends, good coffee, good business deals where everyone leaves feeling successful. I don't want to pick apart all of these things because I know I'm living the life I want and I'm helping others get the things they want. Why would I want to start thinking about what I need? What the hell does that mean for me? What does it mean for my kids after I'm dead and gone?

I wasn't feeling especially thirsty for a different drink, but then comes in this woman who seems to know about some sort of special elixir and she made me wonder. She made me question. Actually, she made me hungry. I thought I just had to know what people wanted—what I wanted. But now, is it worth thinking about what people need—what I need?

★★

AMIE: 'ON SCHEDULE'

Even in my dreams I'm getting things in order—lining up what needs to get done. The trouble is the list of 'things' just keeps growing, even though I'm working as fast as I can. If I could just get everything in place, I could breathe a bit and appreciate it all.

Here's my schedule: on Sundays I make the menu for the week, or at least four days of it, shop and cook what's needed for Monday through Thursday, refrigerate Monday and Tuesday's meals and freeze things for Wednesday and Thursday. Fridays are pizza or leftovers. I try to keep a basket of snacks for my kids' school lunches every day but it always seems to run out early. Theoretically, dinners need to be ready to be finished or defrosted with not more than 20 minutes of prep, but that doesn't always pan out either. I'll do four loads of laundry on Sunday—sometimes five. The outfits for my two school-aged kids are all set because of their uniforms, but on Fridays they wear what they want and my daughter is so self-conscious about looking 'right'—I need to have options ready so she has a choice and doesn't melt down completely before school. My son doesn't care about anything but his shoes. The shoes can't look old he says—which is not a major challenge since his feet grow like weeds and we keep buying him the next pair needed before the last pair gets even mildly worn. The toddler is a day-by-day challenge, because she has a mind of her own.

My husband tries to help, but he commutes to work and has to leave at 6:45 in the morning and doesn't return until after 6 at night. Long day for him but it feels longer for me because I don't have an extra set of hands around to help me get things done. Mondays through Fridays are basically the same. At 5:45 a.m., my youngest wakes me up after a ragged night's sleep. While I would love to exercise to keep my sanity, it never seems possible with all-the-getting-ready-to-start-the-day duties. Just trying to get everyone else up, dressed, fed and ready for school and work (including doing what I need for myself around the edges) feels like a mini-marathon.

Through my constant but loving pressure, intermingled with some minor (and occasional major) tirades, everyone is out the door and on their way to work, school or day care by 7:35 a.m. Part of the secret is that I have the clocks set 7 minutes ahead of schedule which prompts everyone to move with a little bit of urgency and which gets them to their destinations about 2 minutes early. My daily pledge to myself is to keep calm and carry on—sometimes I'm successful.

My oldest daughter gets to the bus on her own and is pleased not to be seen with her parents or siblings. My husband takes my son each day and they both miraculously show up where they're supposed to be—fully dressed and with some idea of what day it is. I like to think their shirts are tucked in and they haven't yet stained some article of clothing. This delusional vision brings me comfort and even makes me smile.

As for me, I head off to drop the toddler at day care and take my youngest daughter to the elementary school where she's a student and I'm a teacher. If we get to school before the first bell at 8:00 a.m., then my daughter does a little homework in my classroom or helps me get ready for the day. It's a sweet time and I think she's proud of me and feels like a special kid, which of course she is. A couple minutes before 8:00 a.m., she heads off to her room and I continue to greet the kids as they sleepwalk into my classroom. I've got my class of kids from 8:00 a.m. until 2:30 p.m. and believe me, I know where those children need to be at every minute. We divide the day into seven periods in which I get 20 minutes for lunch and two 30-minute 'planning periods'. My planning includes going to the bathroom and looking in the mirror to ensure I don't have magic marker stains on my pants or fingerprints on my shirt. Throughout the day, I'm teaching the kids math, reading, science, writing, social studies and more. I get them to and from the gym, art and music rooms. It's ironic that parents hate it when we take a day here and there for professional development because they think we must have time for learning and working together during the regular school day and week. I'd like to give them a math lesson on the time it takes to prep, grade, walk, pee and discipline the three kids who have no sense of their bodies or the garbage that comes out of their mouths. But, overall, I love my job and all the kids in my classroom and I want what's best for them, so I prepare for them like they were my own, which they are.

My daughter comes back to my class a little after 2:30 p.m. We take five minutes to talk about our days. I love that time. Then I grade papers, prepare for class the next day and get the room back in order so it's ready to go for the following school day. I never get everything done by the time I have to go home and I'm usually in serious trouble because it means staying up late that night, which leaves me feeling wiped out for the next day. At 3:45 p.m., it's time to pick up the toddler from day care and my son from his study hall and get him to his sports practice. We drop him off at 4:00 p.m., do errands until 5:15 p.m. and get home at 5:30 p.m. I get the house back in order, finish preparing the meal so that we can all eat at 6:00 p.m. I insist that we all eat together and get appropriately angry at my husband if he can't manage to pick up our son from practice and be at the dinner table on time. We eat from 6:15–6:45 p.m., or at least that's the goal. The kids want to leave the table early, but I try to stretch it because they'll all be grown and gone before we know it. It's important to talk and just be with each other.

Clean-up and sorting out the day is finished by 7:15 p.m., homework gets done, maybe a phone call to my mother, maybe a touch-up to some room that looks like a mess. The kids start going to sleep and we help them from about 7:30 p.m. for the youngest until 9:30 p.m. for the oldest. I sometimes think about single mothers and I'm ready to bow down to them in awe. There's an insane amount of things to do and it never stops.

I start winding down and getting ready for bed, ideally by 10:00 p.m., but that never happens. I inevitably have to finish some grading or prep for the next day or plan for some committee I'm on at school, wash out a stain or help my teenage daughter through the latest crisis. I don't mean to make light of her crises—I've had plenty of my own—but it all takes time. Anyway, I'm usually in bed by 11:00 p.m. and have to read in order to have some chance of falling asleep before 11:30 p.m.

Our weekends seem to be filled with leftover laundry, errands that have to be run, chores around the house, scheduled activities for the kids and, if we are lucky, a family fun outing. My husband and I always talk about exercising and taking a bit of time for ourselves but rarely does that happen given the 'necessary' to-do list and last minute projects. Sometimes, I wonder how our marriage can survive such a deluge of constant shoulds and musts, and I worry that we will regret the coulds. I think I'll feel like I could have done more—that I missed opportunities. It makes me think of that saying about not seeing the forest amidst the trees. I imagine never looking up and missing the joyfulness of the whole picture in front of me.

Sometimes I dream about the lives of other women in far-off lands. I picture the Saudi woman who has her life well protected and cared for by all the men in her life—first her father and brothers, then her husband and sons, though I know the trade-offs are severe. I envision the Australian woman who knows how to farm herself, can put her husband in his place when needed and breathes in deeply the fresh air and the wholesome hearty goodness of life. Or I smile at the delicate French sophisticate who sips her wine, knows her art history and has admiring men to feed her fancies. But I don't let myself wander amidst these stereotypical fantasies for long. Who am I kidding? Those women out there—they're wondering where their time goes just like I do. They're all yearning just like me.

Let me be clear—I am not complaining. I'm proud of all that I accomplish and that I've got a family that's in reasonably good shape. It's just, well, what happens if I do all of the right things, and then I open my eyes, and I'm old. Worn. Wistful. What if I spend all my time now trying to catch my breath, and then when I have time, my life has mostly been determined. I've done all the right things, but I don't feel quite right. My husband says it's a fear of sleepwalking through life and he's ready to shake things up at any time. But that's easy for him to say—he doesn't get that without a schedule, all of our lives would fall apart. I'm working hard to make the dream of a good life come true. I just hope I'm not completely worn out and used up before I can fully enjoy all that's around me and in me. I want to appreciate today and every day—not just schedule it or wish it away.

★★

AARUSH: 'EVERYTHING NOT NOTHING'

I have everything and nothing all figured out. Before I die, I will have lived in seven countries, had three amazing love affairs, failed in one business and succeeded in two, given a million rupees to charity, solved a mystery, been in one Bollywood film, read and understood the philosophies of five world religions (and lived out the practices of at least two of them) and have two kids—both smarter than me.

I read about the American John Goddard's life list. He's the guy who at age 15 wrote his audacious list about the 127 things he wanted to accomplish in his lifetime, and then he spent the next 75 years accomplishing almost all of the things he set out to do. That's awesome; I am going to be like John. I am not going to be like all those wannabes who have a bucket list and then kick the bucket before doing much more than take a photo in front of the Taj or learn how to say hello and goodbye in eight languages. I am not going to live a life that can be described in a one paragraph obituary.

My life will have meaning—whatever that means. Maybe I'll spend a year on a sailboat and write love songs, teach myself to play the sitar and serenade some Arabian beauty. Maybe I'll hang out in a rainforest and keep eating plants until I discover the cure for crazy suicidal tendencies that so many lunatics in the world clearly suffer from. Actually, one of the things I really want to do is write a children's book. Why? Because a really good children's book could change the world. Think about what it could be like to get every kid around the globe to dream higher dreams and believe in the impossible. Yeah, that's where the sweet spot of success really lies—it's transformation on steroids without any health risk.

My first children's book will be about belly button lint. Imagine a kid who decided at age 6 to start saving his belly button lint. He saves that lint for the next 27 years and creates the largest belly button lint ball on the planet. He gets in the *Guinness Book of World Records* and tours the world with his amazing lint ball. People ask him how and why he saved his belly button lint and he gets into crazy discussions about saving useless stuff that will save the world. He says his belly button lint can provide super-efficient insulation for environment-friendly homes. He inspires others to save seemingly useless things.

Soon after learning about the prince of lint, people start saving banana peels to create slicker playground slides which make kids happier and grow up with less junk sticking to them. Other folks begin taking mango pits and making paper plates and bowls out of them which can be rubbed into skin after the food is all eaten. The mango paper disintegrates warts and wrinkles so everyone ends up planting more mango trees and successful side businesses pop up for removing mango strands from in between teeth. There's so much mango success that the GDP of mango growing countries soar and the citizens rejoice in their new-found juice-filled lives. Following closely in the footsteps of the belly button lint idea, senior centers filled with octogenarians, nonagenarians and centurions start collecting the crust from their eyes which turns out to be the secret to the fountain of youth. They bottle the stuff, make millions and every year pick another species facing extinction to live long and prosper.

I have a hard time thinking up ideas that don't involve food waste or body excretions, but it doesn't matter. Kids will get my thinking and they'll tell their teachers to go jump in a lake anytime instructions are given to color all leaves green or all skies blue. They'll say they read Aarush's book and it taught them there's more than one right answer...more than just one way of doing things. Ha! So there!

Computers don't impress me, by the way, but the stuff coming off social media has got to be consumed in a more coherent way. I can invent a social media synthesizer. One stream of unending information bottled in a microchip that's inserted under the ear and gets accessed by the brain on an as-needed basis. I don't have time to waste, nor do most other 20-year-old guys like me who are ready for anything. Get me that chip and it will get rid of a lot of my confusion that's on high speed. In fact, the confusion is going to make me jump off a bridge without a bungee cord because I don't know which way is up and I might as well get a rush on the way out.

Getting a rush and being in a rush are obviously two very different things. I want to get a rush by experiencing lots of different things in my life, but I don't want to be in a rush to get to the other side. The whole rush thing makes me remember a dream I keep having. I dream that I've learned how to walk in the clouds. I run lightly from cloud to cloud—I'm not quite floating but almost swimming like a seahorse, keeping upright, sometimes wavering but never falling. I'm sure this recurring dream has some deep significance and I hope it all means that someday I can fly from place to place without paying any airfare.

Look, I could get more serious and explain that I just finished two years of college and am trying to figure out what job I'm going to get to help my family. Or I could mention that what I'm really thinking about is how to go on an adventure without telling anyone where I'm headed. Why have I been given the challenge of figuring out all the puzzle pieces and reassuring everyone that my life is all set? 'Become an engineer, marry the girl we have found for you, respect family tradition.' That's what I keep hearing, but in my mind, despite the respect I have for my parents, I'm really thinking it's a pile of cow dung that I'm not interested in. If I tried to figure everything out now all at once, I would start spinning around until my head popped off, rolled down the street and clogged up the sewer pipe which would cause a major flood on my street. Then I'll really be in trouble.

Okay, wait. I know I have to slow down and make sure my heart isn't beating too fast. When I can sense my heart beating, I get freaked out. There's too much spinning in my head—too many directions to turn—too much good stuff—or maybe too much bad. My family thinks I must be the one who will know what to do. My cousin even says I'm everyone's ticket forward. I'll be the engineer who figures out how all the pieces fit together and all the money can come flowing in.

But I need a secret decoder bandana to wrap around my brain and make sense out of the chaos. I need a magic potion of belly button lint, banana peels, mango pits and eye crust to give me the protection, quickness, happiness and ability to fend off warts so that I can deal with all the stuff zooming at me. I need all of this stuff plus a map—because I don't want to get off stride, and I don't want to get lost. Also, I want to be sure to experience everything, but not have nothing in the end.

★★

ALIYAH: 'READY TO INVEST'

I've worked hard to get where I am. Since my first days as an accounting intern to my current role as chief financial officer (CFO) for a mid-size company, I earned my position and then some. There are not many women who have accomplished what I have. I am proud of the path I've taken and what I have achieved.

My workdays are no longer filled with profit and loss statements or accounts receivables and payables. I have people who do those day-to-day tasks and they do them well or they end up going elsewhere. (And to be clear, I take good care of the people who work for me—it's just that there's not much room for error when charged with overseeing a company's finances.) Rather than the sometimes brain-numbing role of keeping the books in order, I am now more focused on the sustainable growth of our business.

I think what's made me successful as a CFO is that I balance being a hawk with expenses while maintaining an understanding that we need to make sound investments to grow. When the boys on our executive team start fantasizing about their latest scheme that's sure to make us into a Fortune 500 company within three years, I just ask them some straightforward strategy and financing questions to help bring them back to reality. But when someone comes up with a well thought out idea that stretches our capacity but won't break us if staged sensibly, well, then I'm likely to lend my support and encouragement. Maybe it's my intuition coming through, but I really enjoy nurturing a good venture when I see one.

I know that some middle managers in my company question my skills. But I think they have little or no evidence to support their opinions. And more importantly, instead of paying attention to the doubters, I remember what my father told me. He said that I was smart and capable, and could accomplish anything I wanted in life. He kept telling me, 'Aliyah, always persevere', and that's what I've done.

I've become confident and successful enough in my job that I get asked to sit on panels at conferences and large business meetings. I always try to convey three key lessons. First, I talk about the importance of developing an expertise and ability to interpret and analyze facts rather than just regurgitating them. Second, I explain the knack of knowing how to read between the lines of what people say in relation to what the facts demonstrate. It's a variation on my first piece of advice but this one highlights for leaders the value of being able to listen to people, understand their motives and then determine if the case being made is primarily conjecture or sound logic. Sometimes, I lose people between my first two points, but the more sophisticated in the audience seem to get it, and the women especially like inferring that it takes a little intuition mixed with know-how to be truly savvy.

My third and final point is more blunt: Don't get caught up in a work life to impress others—rather, get caught up in an impressive life that works for you and works for others. In other words, find a path that enables you to be comfortable in your own skin and feeds the people and communities in your life that matter to you. Follow your head, heart and values—then you're more than halfway home.

I make that last point as a way of sharing some wisdom so the young women (and young men, of course) in the audience don't get caught up in trying to prove themselves to others—striving for lives that appear to have the trappings of success, but also the pitfalls of hollowness or misalignment. What would happen, I sometimes ask, if we all pursued lives defined by ambition but also lives that ultimately get restrained by golden handcuffs of 'success' that are not easily unlocked.

I don't want to sound preachy when making my point about living a life that matters. And yet, it seems like a worthwhile point on which to spend some time. And who am I kidding anyway? I make the last point because I have a growing sense that I am now at risk of not following my own advice. I have been through enough in life to recognize when there's something missing—and my missing piece seems right at my fingertips. If I speak out loud about the truth of this major area of risk, maybe I can determine how to account for it in my life. Perhaps this is just my way of checking and balancing my own spreadsheet so I don't go under. Or maybe it's my way of leaving a legacy to those who have looked up to me, or for those who didn't have a father like mine.

Before getting too consumed with the possible deficits in my life, I'm not about to toss aside the pride I have in my professional successes. I'm proud of my career path, plain and simple. But still, now I'm just at the point of thinking, can I have 'both and' instead of 'either or'? Can I have the successful career, but also leverage all that I have learned to become more fully aligned in every aspect of my life? Do I have to cast aside my hard-earned professional stature to discover an existence where my ability and yearning to nurture can blossom beyond the balance sheet?

I sense there's more to life and want to live it all to the lees. I think I have a good deal more power to harness but just need to get a handle on how to work the reigns in a more elevated fashion. It's not about work-life balance for me, it's about integrating the varied and powerful aspects of who I am. It's about understanding why I'm headed in a certain direction, and then having a strong, positive impact on others through a life that's clear and true.

It's funny, particularly for an accountant, now that I've found some solid success, I think I might want to risk it all. Maybe that's crazy and it doesn't have to be all or nothing. But I'll tell you, when you reach the pinnacle of your profession or the top of your personal game, I think that's the same time when you realize you're capable of more. It's not conceit, it's a desire to align everything you have learned so far in life and really do your part to lift up your friends, your loved ones, your community and your world. You get to a point when you realize there's a lot you don't know, but you also have a belief in your ability to observe, interpret and assess the pieces. You have the means to seek the ends for a greater good.

I want my net worth to be more than the sum total of my bank accounts. I have been flying high for several years now; I'm pretty sure that I'm on the precipice of something new. I'm ready to take some risks because I have the wherewithal to get up after a fall. Perhaps the executive summary is that I'm ready to make a thoughtful investment in myself and I'm ready to let go of my current state so that I can step into a new possibility. In the future, I want to sit on a panel and not have to present pearls of wisdom. I want to sit on a panel and present myself. I want my actions, decisions, impacts and journey to all speak for themselves. I want my life to be my message.

LEARNING EXPEDITIONS

It's time to pause. What did you think of the group of people you just met? We introduced you to these individuals to raise your antennae for the journey ahead. You will get to know more about them in the upcoming chapters as they help you connect with the ideas presented. These intriguing acquaintances will provide you with greater access to the tools, models, theories and real-life leaders described in this book.

Indeed, being a keen observer is good and often necessary, but if you're aiming for personal and professional transformation, it's not enough. For such important and impactful learning, you need to engage and experience things for yourself. Towards this end, you will be asked to participate in several 'learning expeditions' throughout this book. The expeditions will allow you to experience and personalize what you have been reading. It will be up to you to start making these pages real by venturing out on the expeditions offered. Do the work. Struggle. Have fun. Don't take yourself too seriously. Grow. Repeat.

EXPEDITION 1: THE MOST IMPORTANT STORY IS YOUR OWN

Remember This One Thing

Badger said:

> I would ask you to remember this one thing. The stories people tell have a way of taking care of them. If stories come to you, care for them. And learn to give them away where they are needed. Sometimes a person needs a story more than food to stay alive. That is why we put these stories in each other's memory. This is how people care for themselves.
>
> —Barry Lopez, *Crow and Weasel*

Robert Coles (1990) wrote about 'the call of stories' and how we move directly from stories into our own lives. Whatever story you hear calling to you is surely something worthy of making you sit up and take note. And ultimately, it's important to remember that the most important story is your own. What is your story that you have created to take care of yourself?

Think about yourself in the current context:

How would you describe your approach to living life and interacting with others?

What courage are you called upon to engage to make it through?

What lenses frame your thinking and perspective?

What guides your ways of being and doing?

What questions do you find that you keep asking yourself?

Stop now and write a few pages in response to these questions—tell your own unique tale. Next, sit back and read your reflections and ponder a bit about the current message your life is telling the world. Share your story with a friend or mentor, and listen to their interpretation of your story. What did you learn about your own everyday profile in courage?

TIME TO ACT: HOW WILL YOU RESPOND?

Stories are a good place to start. Stories help give context, touchstones and frameworks to understand others' perspectives and your own. They give depth and breadth to the journeys people are on, and they demonstrate how there is so much richness and texture in people's lives that no one can be reduced to an executive summary or a footnote. Telling your own story can help you make sense out of seemingly conflicting feelings and thoughts, and eventually help you sew a coherent thread through the pieces that form the fabric of your existence. When you reflect upon your story, you allow yourself to look at how past experiences inform your future. Stories, however, do not always propel you into the future. They do not always challenge you to leap forward. Invitations, on the other hand, entice you into the unknown. Invitations help you to explore. Invitations cause you to decide and to act.

You were greeted with three invitations at the beginning of the book. Now that you have recognized your own unique story, it's time to RSVP to your invitation.

EXPEDITION 2: YOUR RSVP

The hero's journey often starts with a bit of resistance to the call for adventure. You can certainly stop right now and determine that the initial story you wrote about yourself was good, acceptable...enough for now. Perhaps the timing is not right, you have too many other things to do, or things in your life are truly on the right track and fulfilling. What a wonderful place to be—please do stick with your story and let it keep unfolding. Or if the timing is simply not good right now, you're already feeling too raw, too fragile, too much in danger, then maybe you can choose the invitation you want to hold onto. There's no expiration date, no hard and fast deadline by which to respond. Put the invitation in a safe place, remember where it is, check it out now and then, and answer the call when you're ready.

However, if you have decided now is the time to accept, then take a moment and write a short RSVP. Consider what has captivated you so far. Why have you kept reading these initial pages? Could you see a bit of yourself in one of the initial profiles shared in the opening of this book? Did you read one of the invitations and think to yourself, 'Yes, I'm curious about the answers to some of those questions. Yes, I'm experiencing some of those thoughts and feelings. Yes, I sense I'm capable of more—more belief and pride in myself, more positive influence and engagement with others, more impact and significance within the communities where I live and work.' Explain which invitation you're responding to and why this feels like the right time for you to engage. Note down the words, logic or sentiments that caught your attention and compelled you to say, yes, I accept. I'm in.

COME IN, COME IN: WHOEVER YOU ARE

Whether you're a wanderer who has a general sense that it's time to start searching, or if you're among the dubious who simply welcomes straight talk about a path forward, or if you're already committed and feeling ready to live life to the fullest—it doesn't really matter once you have accepted the invitation...you're in.

Accepting the invitation to thrive, empower, serve, transcend and lead is a good and important first step forward towards living a full and impactful life. But accepting the invitation only means you found the open door for discovering your life's greatest calling. You found an on-ramp from wherever you currently exist. Sometimes wanderers accidently find an entrée point because they're comfortable with being lost and found. Sometimes the dubious are propelled forward because they are driven to discover the most efficient and effective means to power ahead toward their goals. And for those already committed—well, they inevitably find a way forward because of their deep sense that there is simply more of themselves ready to be discovered. Whatever driving force propelled you and enabled you to accept this invitation—grab hold of it. Use the power you have to get started, and then harness the power you gain to keep you moving onward.

CHAPTER 2

WHY YOU, WHY NOW?

About Our Current Context That Calls for a Different You and a Different Us

Now that you have considered the invitations and determined that you are in, we would also like you to consider a larger context for why it's time that more of us say 'yes' and, more specifically, why the power of your yes is so critically important. While it is true that this is a journey most meaningfully taken through your own very personal lens, we'd like to offer a prequel that creates a more connected context for you and others who will join you. Clearly, investing in ourselves not only pays dividends for our individual future but ultimately, and maybe even more importantly, for those we influence. The possibility of expanding our collective ability to lift up society as a whole is not only enticing but essential, given our current human condition. So test your resolve and take a cold, hard look at the present to understand more completely what is at stake in our collective commitment to respond with a full-throated 'yes'.

HOW DID WE END UP HERE?

To take the long view, our complex human journey has taken us from simple tribal connections and interdependence on each other and on the earth to complex urban societies that have fostered independence, separation and increased competition for resources. More specifically, over our collective history, indigenous people around the world have been uprooted, displaced and enslaved by dominant cultures in the name of religion, modernity and commerce. And while we have gained important scientific advances, mind-blowing technologies and nearly tripled longevity, it has come at a steep price: losing sight of the once held deep connectedness to each other and to Mother Nature who provides our food, shelter and clothing. There are overwhelming signs that we have become less concerned with relationships that our collective humanity has been devalued and so disconnected to Planet Earth that even our current best efforts to save her are sorely lacking. Our people are crying out for respect and dignity, and our once abundant land is thirsty, hungry and in need of tender loving care like never before.

As author Margaret Wheatley and others who hold a dystopian view of the current state note, we are now members of a highly technological society that has created a world where only very few hold power, where income disparity has increased exponentially, where there is danger of destroying our planet in search of short-term profit, and where disconnected communities are willing to go to war with each other in the name of religious fervour, righteous claims and fear of mutual destruction. Taken together, these results are clearly linked to command and control, power-over leadership run amuck with greed, self-interest and short-sightedness.

If you think about more examples closer to home in your place of work, it's most likely easy to recognize decreased human and economic resources, stagnated wages and a diminished respect for our foundational institutions of government, health care and education. Correspondingly, we have seen an increase in global competition, customer and collegial diversity, technological expectations and an overall demand to 'do more with less'. It's no wonder that these combined factors have fostered a weakened sense of our ability to do the work and, as a result, our sense of efficacy. Efficacy is a combination of competence and confidence that a job well done can be accomplished. Without efficacy, a workforce can become apathetic, inefficient and demoralized. We've all seen instances where work has become overwhelming and almost undoable. However, when efficacy is high, energy, engagement and successful outcomes are the norm.

The contrasting examples of two very different school superintendents make the point. A mid-career school leader, we'll call him Sam, was recently hired from a smaller school district to take over a larger and more prestigious district. This was the job of a lifetime and one that he wanted to retain at all costs. Consequently, his leadership style became one of divide and conquer, micromanagement and creating a culture of fear. He even told his administrative team that his leadership role model was Attila the Hun! It wasn't long before principals and teachers began to understand that speaking up and taking risks was not safe in the new environment. To make matters worse, they were specifically told that if they tried something new and it failed, he would not be there to support them. It wasn't long before morale plummeted, and the efficacy of long-time school employees was severely diminished. Their new mantra? 'Watch your back, keep your head down and try to survive.' It's no wonder that student performance began to suffer and the toxic leadership eventually led to a toxic school culture.

Contrasted to Sam is Elaine. She was hired as superintendent in the same school district she had served as a principal. She was known for building a culture of collaboration, shared knowledge creation and a focus on what works best for student achievement. Her strong relationships, heavy investment in professional development and 'can do' outlook endeared her to parents, students and staff. Everyone began to feel that they could and would make a real difference in the quality of student learning and ultimately achievement results followed. Whether these leadership behaviors occur in schools or in businesses or non-profits, the results are likely the same. A CEO who creates a culture of fear and inhibits innovation or a non-profit leader who minimizes employee autonomy though micromanagement will lead to decreased employee efficacy and bottom line results. Conversely, business and non-profit leaders who value and empower their employees will no doubt reap the benefits of human capital that is high in efficacy and heavily invested in the success of the enterprise.

Given the stresses of the complexities of life in the 21st century, evident internally in our workplaces and externally in our environment, a more advanced and enlightened type of leadership is clearly needed. Something else is surely possible beyond the type of leadership influence that pushes down from above. Elaine and leaders like her begin to show us the way.

REMEMBER THE TORNADO?

FIGURE 2.1 THE DOWNWARD SPIRAL OF COMMAND AND CONTROL LEADERSHIP

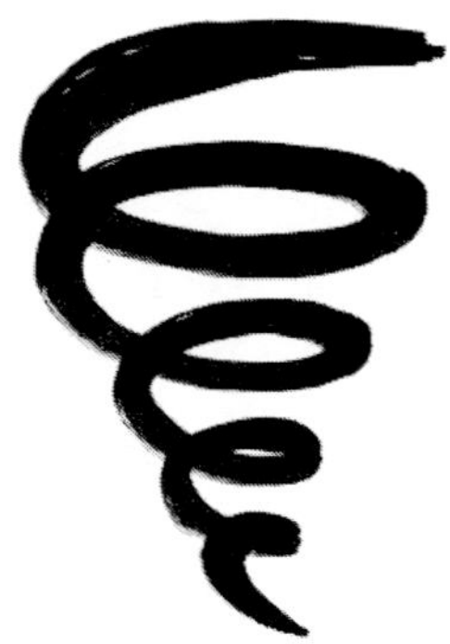

Source: Nick Blair

When a tornado arrives, the fearsome tornadic forces push down and create a path of destruction, wreaking havoc on the Earth and any objects or beings in its path. A tornado is fueled by absorbing all the energy around it in order to become more powerful—larger, faster and more awe-inspiring. As a metaphor for leadership, this represents command and control, a top-down leadership model (as depicted in Figure 2.1) mainly interested in gathering more power and resources, oblivious to the chaos or destruction that results, either as a predetermined or unintended consequence. And as with tornadoes, such leadership is not sustainable because energy eventually subsides when it has taken all there is to be had.

Some prognosticators warn of the destruction of our environment and the resources upon which we depend, accompanied by the breakdown in relationships between hostile societies, economic decline and accompanying political schisms that make it nearly impossible to solve problems. The common thread of past failed societies is that collapse happens rapidly as it approaches its peak (think Mayan culture, Nazi Germany, the Soviet Union, Easter Island). Since our present course is not sustainable, nor conscionable, isn't it clear we must move past our current way of solving problems through greed, self-interest and the desire for power? Must we not invest in a more productive, generous, compassionate and life-giving means of influence?

These problems in our societies and our workplace are of our own making and must be solved by our own hands. While negative views of the present can be both alarming and disheartening, and we should look at the realities of the collective trajectory of our human condition, never should we gaze upon the future without hope. By examining our progression with clear eyes, we also have the opportunity to take advantage of our own ingenuity. Luckily, we humans have an amazing capacity to survive, to innovate and to create when times get the toughest.

A great example of corporate ingenuity and responsible environmental stewardship can be found in Unilever, the Dutch-British consumer goods company. CEO Paul Polman came to the company in 2009 and created a shift to become a steward of the environment and a more socially responsible business by implementing what was called the Sustainable Living Plan. Under his leadership, Unilever committed to the 100 percent use of renewable energy across all of its operations by 2030, and as by 2019 already reduced emissions by 43 percent. New products that reduce water or energy use this approach to engage customers in protecting the environment as well. Shareholders were initially sceptical, but those who stuck with the company were rewarded with a return on investment vastly superior to the FTSE index and that of rivals such as Nestlé.

The highly regarded organizational development guru Peter Drucker famously said 'culture eats strategy for breakfast,' and Polman apparently agreed. He fended off a takeover attempt by Kraft Heinz, a deal that would have been a near-term win for investors but would have set up a clash of diametrically opposed corporate cultures. Polman's actions speak louder than words, but his words were pretty impressive as well when he explained in a *Financial Times* podcast, 'True leadership is putting yourself to the service of others and, if you can marry that with a very noble cause, to make this a better place for all.' Leaders like Polman give us hope and create a standard for courage and creativity in the face of adversity.

THE ALTERNATIVE BETTER CASE

With all the challenges that are before us, there is ample evidence that all is not lost. Indeed, signs of hope, promise and possibility are abundant. In many parts of the world, social justice is finding a voice through a shift in both thinking and action that was once inconceivable. The subjugation of one race to another, of women in the workplace, of classism and homophobia, are lessoning at historically rapid rates. Consider the following:

- There is a growing rediscovery of the interrelatedness between people and the planet.
- There is decrease in ego among a growing number of people, creating a movement towards benevolence and collective responsibility.
- Some large corporations are beginning to understand that our present level of income disparity is not sustainable.
- There is a growing appreciation of how education and entrepreneurism are the tickets out of poverty and towards sustainable wealth generation.

As Eckhart Tolle tells us, 'acute crises and dysfunction always precedes or coincides with any evolutionary advancement or gain in human consciousness.' (Tolle, 2008). We all need adversity to evolve—otherwise what would be the impetus?

We have asked you to consider the current context of our environment and our workplaces not to discourage you but to fuel your imagination about the tremendous opportunity we have right here and right now. By using your ability to imagine what does not now exist, but possibly could be realized for both yourself and your community, you can create the possibility of the better case scenario.

This is a unique human ability as far as we know, the ability to live in the present and also transcend it to think of the future. It is this very ability that has allowed us to create soaring symphonies, heart filling poetry, inspired artistic expression and mind-blowing technologies. As a matter of fact, it's most likely that as you are reading this you are thinking about how these words connect to what you have learned in the past, ring true to your understanding of the present and perhaps propel you to begin asking the question 'so what next?' Your amazing brain holds the power to iteratively conceive of the past and the present while projecting into the future in nanoseconds of rapid processing.

We are now asking you to imagine a different kind of human interaction that stands in sharp contrast to the trail of power and control leadership ingrained in the progression of human history. We define leadership, powerfully and simply, as a process of influence to achieve a goal. By this definition, anytime you are in a relationship with another you have the opportunity to influence the outcome, whether it be which movie you will see, which car to purchase or which business transaction to make. It is the character of the influence that makes all the difference. Also by definition, leadership is not a title at all—haven't you known people with a title and no influence, and conversely people without a title but a great deal of influence? It is indeed within the realm of each of us to move away from the powerful destructive forces of command and control leadership, towards a more open, compassionate and generative type of influence—one that transforms our relationships and society for the better, that emanates from clear core values and is aligned to the contribution that is uniquely ours to make.

EXPEDITION 3: REVERSING YOUR INFLUENCE

Take a moment to think about real-world examples from your current life at work or at home that have been negatively affected by command and control decision-making. Think about your own workplace and what it would be like, feel like and look like under the old top-down leadership model. Then use your brilliant imagination to determine what an alternative leadership influence, one that aims to serve, might look like and result in.

Command and Control Influence	**Look, Feel, Be Like**	**Leadership That Serves Influence**	**Look, Feel, Be Like**
Holds on to power *Thinks they have the answers* *Plays it close to the vest* *Divides and conquers* *Is invested in self-aggrandizement and self-advancement* *Uses 'tit for tat' transactions*		*Focused on the best interest of the others, not themselves* *Clear about values and purpose* *Insures alignment of values and purpose through the organization (coherence)* *Courageous about non-negotiables* *Passionate about empowering those they serve*	

ELEVATING SELF AND SYSTEMS

FIGURE 2.2 ASCENDING SPIRAL OF TRANSFORMATIONAL LEADERSHIP

Source: Nick Blair

As you have just demonstrated with your examples, we must turn the traditional tornadic force upside down and begin to cultivate and support those of us who choose to influence, so we see ourselves in service to those we lead. Now, as never before, surviving, more importantly thriving, depends on it. This type of leader is in the business of elevating self, others and the systems they influence. This leader first elevates self by examining and developing motivation, purpose and skill to successfully serve—making a commitment to the ascending spiral of the who, why, what and how questions you have agreed to answer (as depicted in Figure 2.2). Additionally, this leader elevates others by discovering the brilliance within and furthering capacity to collaborate and innovate. And finally, this leader is concerned with elevating systems to dynamic and effective interconnections that can adapt fluidly to the changes needed and desired. The combined effect of such a higher leadership ideal, empowering, engaging and entrusting the hard work to others, magnifies the upward progression of power, from bottom to top. All rise with this model of leadership, all become clearer, stronger and more capable of creating the significant changes needed to save our communities, our organizations, our planet and ourselves.

Mary Barra, the CEO of General Motors (GM) is such a leader. Three months into her tenure she faced multiple investigative hearings before the US Congress for defective ignition switches on thousands of GM vehicles. There were 13 people who died as a result of this devastating manufacturing mistake. Even though all of this happened before she was CEO, Barra immediately and masterfully handled the crisis by expressing genuine compassion for the victims, transparency with investigators and a commitment to creating a new company culture that would produce the best autos within its competitive classes. Her pledge to get to the root of the problem, create transparency, break down company silos and instill shared responsibility changed the direction of GM's corporate culture.

Barra knew that a big change was necessary, and that relationships were the key to eradicating systemic dysfunction. Her goals for the company shifted from being the biggest to being the best by stressing quality at every level. In an interview with CNN, she is quoted as saying, 'Your company culture should empower and inspire people to relentlessly pursue the company's vision—always with integrity.'[1]

As the examples of Mary, Paul and Elaine all illustrate, the past is gone. We cannot retrace our collective human evolution and modify either the glory or the inglorious. The future hasn't arrived, so spending time fantasizing about either the worst or best case is pointless. So why now? Because it is all that we can individually and collectively influence. And the first and most important person you must influence is yourself. But, why you?

WHY NOT?

Certainly the description of the current state and the monumental shift to a better future may seem overwhelming, so it's only fair for you to be thinking 'what could just one person do? What could I do? Why me?' To be sure, why *should* you embark on this expedition of self-discovery?

---

[1] Retrieved from https://edition.cnn.com/2018/10/05/success/best-executives-traits/index.html and https://www.cnn.com/2018/10/11/success/mary-barra-gm/index.html

You may be familiar with the quote 'If not me, who, if not now, when?' used by former US President Ronald Reagan, speaking of the need to step up and vote for his brand of national reform. The origin of this quote is actually from Rabbi Hillel in the first century BCE, 'If I am not for myself, who is for me? And when I am for myself, what am "I"? And if not now, when?' Hillel's admonition is closer to the potential this book holds for you. He suggests that if you are not going to stick up for yourself, love yourself, trust yourself, then who will? You and only you can be true to yourself. Indeed the person you have the deepest influence on is YOU! The latter half of the quote suggests that neither you nor the world can wait one second longer for you to embark on finding such clarity about your life's meaning and calling. This is nothing less than a call to service—first to self—to elevate self, so that you can be of service to others and to the deity you revere.

Hillel also stated 'what is hateful to you, do not do to your fellow,' which is, of course, an early version of the Golden Rule: a guideline that emanates from all the world's major religions. Taken together, we need waste no more time wondering why we should not invest in drilling down to find our real purpose in life and discovering how we can better conditions for ourselves and others. How can we serve to reverse the destructive tornadic action of command and control leadership? How can we 'pay our rent for the air you breath and the space you inhabit', as Marian Wright Edelman asks? (Edelman, 1993)

And lest you fear that you can't measure up or commit to such a grand notion as saving our planet, serving up social justice to the underserved and creating supportive and productive workplaces, rest assured that no one thinks he or she can do it alone. Everyone asks 'how can one person really make a difference?' And the simple answer is that only one can make a difference when it really matters, and it is the collective ripple effect of many 'ones' who absolutely can shift conditions for the good. Nelson Mandela would never have guessed as he was sitting in prison on Robben Island that upon his release he would become a source of healing and reconciliation to his countrymen, ultimately ending Apartheid. Rich Teerlink would not have guessed that his simple gesture of riding across America to listen to Harley riders was the solution to saving his company.

In all these cases, these leaders didn't really believe initially that they could make a difference, but by being clear about what they valued and their purpose in life, and investing in the uppermost desire to serve, they were able to move proverbial mountains. And so can you. It's a shift in mindset that is required and one, fortunately, that you can achieve.

A SHIFT IN MINDSET

Mindsets are our fundamental set of beliefs about yourself, a way of thinking about what we are able to do. Carol Dweck's research suggests that some people hold a fixed mindset believing that their abilities and attitudes are written in stone and unlikely, if not impossible, to change (Dweck, 2007). This is a terribly self-defeating frame of mind and luckily based upon false premises. A much more productive mindset is one that believes in our ability to develop our talents, skills and attitudes. Not only is this growth mindset firmly rooted in what we know about our brains unlimited ability to develop new connections and even new brain cells over our lifetime, but also clearly demonstrated in recent research about the leaps in learning that occur when we shift to a growth mindset.

What does it mean to shift from a fixed to a growth mindset? Simply put, it means that you make a decision and act upon it. Related to your life's message, it means you shift from the following:

- I don't know who I am *to* I'm really clear about my core values and how they define me. I know that I have the ability to determine when and when I am not in alignment with my values and I have the power to course correct.
- I'm not really clear about my purpose in life *to* I know why I'm here and can clearly state my life's mission. I am convinced that my life will be a coherent journey to live out my purpose.
- I'm unsure about what I want to achieve *to* I not only concretely know what my desired outcomes are but can see myself achieving them.
- I'm worried about my own capabilities to achieve my mission and intended outcomes *to* I am clear, competent

and confident in the many ways that I will use my influence productively to achieve my desired outcomes.

Mindsets can also be dispositional in nature. We've all heard about holding a cup half full versus half empty outlook. If you're a person who gravitates towards seeing the cup half empty rather than half full, a pessimist rather than an optimist, it's likely time for you to consider a mind shift. A simple story illustrates this point:

> A (fictitious) experiment was conducted with children to determine the distinctions that are formed early in one's orientation to life circumstances. The first child was taken into a room filled with shiny new toys and observed. He just stood there frozen, afraid to act. When asked what the problem was, he answered, 'I'm afraid I'll break something.'
>
> Another child was taken into a room filled with manure, piled high. This second child dove into the manure immediately and started digging. When asked what was going on, she replied, 'With all of this manure, I just know there is a pony in here somewhere.'

Whether it is the massive problem of income disparity, the challenges of the competitive marketplace, the overwhelming needs of social welfare and justice, the learning, health or wealth gap between privileged and underprivileged peoples or some other burning issue that drives your mission, leaders must have an optimistic and innovative orientation. Effective leaders are never resigned to the current reality or opt to take a 'this is the best we can do' stance. If the leader doesn't believe that there is a 'pony in there somewhere', who will?

It won't take much for you to look around and see the piles of manure with opportunity waiting to be discovered, whether it's in your life, company, community, educational or health care system, or non-profit organization. You already know that complex problems won't be solved with simple answers, current paradigms and quick fixes. You most likely have tried many of those to little avail.

EXPEDITION 4: IF NOT YOU, WHO? IF NOT NOW, WHEN?

Take a moment to reflect on the following questions related to what's happening within your sphere of influence:

1. The Manure:
   What is not working, not sustainable and/or not productive in your current status quo? Who is not being served that needs to be?
2. The Possibility:
   What do you see as the preferred future—a different way of doing business—a possible outcome for success?
3. The Mind Shift:
   What role do you see for yourself in creating this change? Whether you have positional power or title, or are leading with quiet influence, do you see a way to shift your perception, to step up your influence and to have the courage to make a difference?

The Tibetan Buddhist monk, Chögyam Trungpa, taught, 'Something that is worthwhile, wholesome and healthy exists in all of us. By opening to the world as it is, we may find that gentleness, decency, and bravery are available—not only to us but to all human beings.' (Trungpa, 2014). Armed with an optimistic attitude and an innovative spirit, the answer is simple. You are the leader that your corner of the world has been waiting for. You are the one who can accept the mantle of leadership, not necessarily the title, but more importantly, the influence. You are the one who is willing to fight the good fight and persist to the end. And you are the one who has decided to invest in yourself to prepare for the challenges ahead. Horace Mann, the great American educational reformer, challenged us all by stating,

'Be ashamed to die until you have won some victory for humanity.' It's time for you to define the victory you want to win and to create the path forward to achieving it (Mann, 1989).

The level of commitment that you now more fully understand will require a great deal of focus and intention. This final stage of preparation, described in Chapter 3, supports your ability to bring full presence to this audacious task.

CHAPTER 3

FINDING YOUR PATH TO PRESENCE

About How to Fully Engage in the Journey

In the classic tale of *The Little Prince*, Antoine De Saint-Exupery created the quintessential king of curiosity (De Saint-Exupery, 1943). The little prince had endless questions—continuously in search of the answers he needed for a more fulfilling life. Could a sheep eat the nasty little baobab trees growing on his planet? Could a ruler of the land determine when the sun sets and the stars shine? Could a businessman make things count just by counting them? The little prince genuinely wanted to know the answers to his questions—that's why he asked them.

In the exuberant story of *Zorba the Greek*, Nikos Kazantzakis described a robust man who lived life to the fullest (Kazantzakis, 1952). Zorba approached every aspect of his life with gusto, whether he was overseeing workers in a mine, interacting with mad monks on a mountaintop or making love with the fullness of his being.

Zorba gave life his whole heart and in return expected all the abundant joy that a life worth living should encompass.

In the somewhat more sobering world of Plato's *Apology*, in which Socrates famously reasoned that the 'unexamined life is not worth living', the grand challenge presented was not only to seriously question the wisdom of others but also one's own self-worth (Plato, 2017). Rather than any sort of apology in the modern sense of the word, what Socrates unapologetically suggests is that each of us needs to have enough courage and humility to dig deep within our own minds and hearts, and discern what is real and true about our world, our assumptions and our ways of understanding and being.

The Little Prince, Zorba the Greek and Socrates all have something very important in common. Each found a way to feel fully engaged and present in their lives. The Little Prince knew that by being curious, he could make sense of his environs and find direction. Zorba knew that by putting his full heart into everything he did, he would experience life's treasures deeply, fully and madly. And Socrates knew that by being consciously introspective, he could connect with perhaps the most near and dear critic in his life—himself.

Approaching life with curiosity, heart and internal connectedness and coherence not only make for good storytelling and literature, they are also the most vital ingredients in being able to fully engage in a life of greater clarity and impact. Individuals with these capacities are the ones who have the ability to truly listen to the people around them, to be fully awake in their daily lives and to be true to themselves. There is no better way to start understanding your own *who* then by cultivating the discipline of being present and engaged. If you cannot find a way to be genuinely curious about the world around you, if you don't figure out how to be in relationships and authentically connect with others, and if you don't know what's in your heart and have passion that is fueled by your core, then it's likely you will get lost within the bottom of the ascending spiral and tossed out before you ever really get started on your journey.

If you pause to consider the path of Gio, you find a man yearning to be present and fully engaged in his life. He sensed that his mentors and friends helped him be present through their support, questions and storytelling. He knew that they were truly with him—connected—and he felt the same when in their company. Gio was also able to feel fully alive and present, and recognize those qualities in others when he traveled the world. The tea taster in Darjeeling, the Salvadorian poet and the hospitable Dubai doctor were proof to Gio that there are people in this world who could think and feel deeply, and who could reach out to others in ways that cut through the mundane and the inconsequential. The people Gio encountered were at ease with themselves and so, in turn, he could feel at ease with his own self. But the mentors, supporters and people he met weren't enough to sustain Gio and help him find a way he could maintain presence in all aspects of his life. He knew he had to keep exploring and keep searching for a way of being that was beyond the ordinary; a place that wasn't just fine, but rather, a place where he could retain his curiosity and heart—a place where he felt fully engaged.

Fortunately for Gio, he had enough presence of mind to recognize that he was in reach of something profound and extraordinary. He had tasted and witnessed what it was like to be present and engaged, and he wanted more. He also knew that what he had on a daily basis wasn't sufficient. It just wasn't enough to make up stories about others' lives and not know his own story. Gio could not exactly put his finger on what was missing, but he knew he was not completely whole. He sensed a shift was needed, and that he had to persevere beyond the inertia of everyday life to discover the connectedness and vibrancy that he sought.

Think about Charlie in contrast to Gio. For much of his life, Charlie thought he had all the answers. He boasted that the only thing he had to do to get ahead in life was to figure out what other people wanted and then give it to them. Once you give people what they want, he reasoned, then you get what you want. Charlie was all about transactional relationships, negotiating his way through business deals and career success by paying attention to his customers' interests so that he could ultimately serve his own interests. It wasn't until an acquaintance asked Charlie to take a deeper look at himself that he really stopped for a moment and became real and present. His daily tactics of making deals to get ahead all of a sudden felt hollow and lacking.

Charlie was challenged to take a hard look at whether he was just coasting on the surface of life, but not truly aligning his core values with his decisions and actions. He wasn't fully aware of what he needed for himself, nor if he even really wanted to connect with others. He did ultimately get a wake-up call—one that rocked his world enough to give him a glimpse of what Gio felt deeply. Charlie for the first time realized that it actually might not be sufficient to just maneuver his way to superficial success. He realized that maybe there could be more in life—an acknowledgement he was somewhat reluctant to accept. And an acknowledgement that it was time for some challenging self-examination, even while the thought of the whole process made him wince.

For a guy like Charlie, being fully present was not only difficult, it wasn't even a priority. Further, the conundrum for people like Charlie is that there's minimal awareness of what full presence and connectedness feels like. Gio at least knew the power and significance that being engaged with the self and others can have; Charlie was stuck with being an operator who had no deeply rooted sense of purpose or foundation. Charlie didn't know his *who* and, as a result, was not motivated to engage with others. When you lack clarity about your *who*, it's tougher to be genuinely curious, it's harder to build meaningful connections, and it's unlikely you're able to show your true heart and be real. Until his wake-up call, Charlie lacked authenticity and, as a result, his journey was fairly static. He was at the bottom of the ascending spiral with no access to a path forward, no place to get a foothold and no place to connect.

STEPS FORWARD ON THE PATHWAY

Step 1: Understand How You Connect

There are many ways to consider and understand how to become more present and engaged in our lives. Indeed, it's a realm that philosophers and poets have explored and wrestled with for years. Martin Buber, in sorting out the subtleties of 'I and thou', and trying to decipher the influences of psychology, sociology and religion in living a fuller life, returned to a fundamental truth that 'G-d is in our relationships'. In other words, Buber recognized that when human connection is at its strongest, there is almost an indescribable sense of spiritually present—an uncluttered space of linkage that feels powerful and good. And in terms of the engagement that an invested heart brings, poets like Rainer Maria Rilke let us know that it can take a lifetime to become connected at our cores. 'For one human being to love another', says Rilke, 'that is perhaps the most difficult of all our tasks—for which all other work is but preparation'.

Surely there is a reason why so many have searched for ways of expressing the compelling nature of being present and engaged. Presence is that feeling of being connected to the self and others which is not only empowering, it's precious. When a person gets to that rare state where the world is integrated, aligned and coherent, then there's a realization that there is so much more potential to feel full and whole, to grasp how to truly support and appreciate others and to influence others in positive ways. And yet, while learning about the journeys of others offers a window into the attraction and strength of presence and engagement, it's understanding how to access our own pathways and opportunities for engagement with ourselves and others that matter most. More pointedly, in order to start on our own path forward and venture upwards in the ascending spiral, we must learn how to unleash our own curiosity, open our hearts and fully engage.

Stop here. Forget about Gio and Charlie for the moment. And, as brilliant as they are, set aside the deep contemplations of Buber and Rilke. These references have value in setting the context, in helping to familiarize you with the terrain, but they are not your ticket forward. To be able to discern and progress in your personal path, it's time to start thinking more pointedly about who you are and what support you will need to be curious and connected with your own head and heart. How will you be present?

Part of the answer may be to think of examples of people who you admire for their ability to connect with the world and who clearly feel comfortable in their own skin. Think about the people you have met who care deeply about others and who seem to have found ways to be genuine and authentic in the way they engage. How would you describe their ways of being and interacting? How do you think they have developed their sense of self that it takes to be real and authentic? Perhaps the people you admire experienced loneliness or deep hurt, and then they climbed back up from those raw emotions more determined to make every day matter. Possibly, those you respect found a way to recognize when they felt at peace within themselves, appreciating what felt right and good, and then simply and naturally shared that peace with others. It's helpful to consider the paths of others and how they came to be who they are—but it's not enough. The trick to real presence and engagement, and to move forward on your own journey is to understand the source of your own power. Your true wisdom lies within in your core. Discover it. Reflect upon those times when everything felt in sync for you and imprint those experiences and sensations deep into your memory. Allow your center to emerge and be with others.

EXPEDITION 5: OBSERVING AND PRACTICING PRESENCE

Take the time to write in a journal each day over the course of a week. Write down what high points were experienced and when you felt present. Can you articulate how you felt and why? What was the environment, the connection, the alignment and coherence that was experienced? When did you feel like you had especially strong clarity about what you were hearing from others, or what you were sensing in yourself? Was there a particular reason that you were able to be completely engaged with your environment, your community, your friends, colleagues or family?

Capture what you experienced:

Write it down. Draw it. Take a picture of it.

Hold on to it through whatever means that works for you.

Once you have done this exercise, start thinking about how you can get to that place of presence more frequently. Keep practicing the ways in which you accessed presence, and then keep working to expand the times you're able to realize that way of existing. Presence can be fleeting if you're not consciously focused on how to sustain it. Recognizing how you realize presence and then practicing that way of being can eventually make it an integrated part of who you are.

We were fortunate to interview Paul Durante, a wildly successful technology mogul in Great Britain who discovered that he was most involved, most engaged, most curious and most fulfilled when he volunteered for Habitat for Humanity. He eventually traded in the fast track, the 90-hour work weeks, the bells and whistles that come with great financial success, for the complete connection he felt for the mission of Habitat for Humanity. In the most compelling way, he was drawn to the physical labour in building homes for the homeless and for the opportunity to listen deeply to the stories of those who received them.

When we caught up with Paul, he had become the Director of Habitat for Humanity in South Africa where, through a combination of his business acumen and his clear understanding of the local needs, he was in the process of shifting the vision from home building to community building. As he stated: '…over that period of time in London I kept feeling that there must be something more in life. I explored Buddhism but came back to Christianity and read the Bible in a new way—that there is more to life. I felt like I was seeing through the charade of consumerism and a growing spiritualism changed me.'

It was Paul's ability to be present to his own core values, and determination to align his life to them that created this amazing transformation in his personal mission and the resulting effect it has had on so many lives.

Step 2: Recognize Presence

Presence definitely has a certain feeling to it and perhaps even a look. The progression depicted in Figure 3.1 illustrates what a growing presence looks like.

FIGURE 3.1 THE PROGRESSION OF PRESENCE

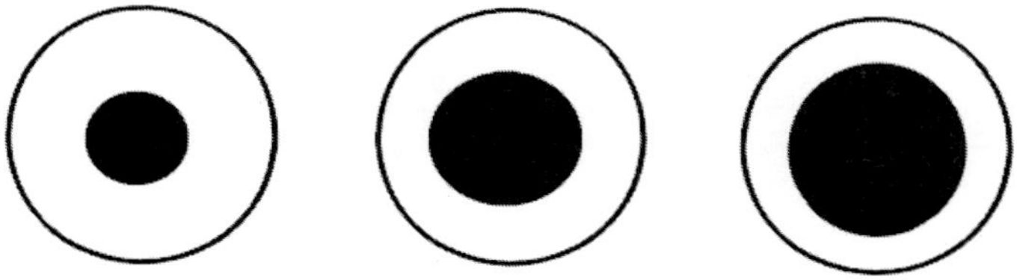

Source: The Authors

In the first open circle, there is only a small filled-in, solid circle. It's a picture of someone's center being far inside and inaccessible. The core is not at all connected to the external world and, as a result, there is a feeling of disconnectedness; a sense of being lost within the self. In this existence, there's so much space between the interior and exterior, between what others (and even the self) are allowed to see, that deep connection is just about impossible. If your *who* is buried deep inside with no pathway out, how can you connect to yourself or with others, and how will others find their way in? You truly are living in the blind spot. Blind to your own self and creating a barrier between you and others.

Figure 3.2 illustrates the inner core growing and beginning to approach the exterior. When you're in these states of being, you begin to have a sense of how you want to be, perhaps a little like Charlie, and maybe like Amie, who was becoming aware that she was missing the 'now'. In these ways of being, there's also sense of the converse of presence—an experience of absence. In the state of absence, there's clearly something missing; something that's difficult to identify but surely a gap that doesn't feel quite right. When there's absence, there's a feeling that your *who* is not really showing up in the world. As the noted scientist and medical doctor Lewis Thomas might say, when there's absence, there's a disturbance in the ecosystem that diminishes your function. Your internal ecosystem is in disequilibrium. You don't exist at full capacity.

You cannot engage fully with yourself or others. Your life is diminished by not being fully awake, fully present.

FIGURE 3.2 ARRIVING AT FULL PRESENCE

Source: The Authors

The growth of presence within and finally a wholly engaged presence are illustrated in Figure 3.2. Aarush and Aliyah are closer to these ways of being. Aarush is so alert and connected to the world, albeit in a somewhat frenetic way, that he wants to connect to everything. Even with his mind racing and creative whirlwind thinking, Aarush shows up as himself. He's someone who is exploring and trying to figure things out. He's not pretending to be someone he's not, rather, he is who he is, trying to decide exactly where to focus his energy so that he can realize his full potential. Aarush's core is close to the surface and he's just about ready to see all the world has to offer, and we can see him for being his lively, imaginative, ready-to-explode self. There's little pretence or hidden agenda with Aarush, so he's more ready to discover and be discovered.

And then there's Aliyah. She's someone who seems to be comfortable in her own skin. She's certainly still evolving, but appears to have arrived at a comfort level that enables her not to be uneasy about what's missing or dwell on what's absent, rather she's happy about the *who* she has grown into, and she simply wants to keep growing, clarifying, connecting and being more impactful. It's likely if you were sitting in the room with a person like Aliyah, you would know she's present with you. You know she has a level of coherence and alignment of her values and actions that allows her to connect the pieces within herself, to connect with you, to enable her to feel at home wherever she is because her *who* is so solid. When you're at a place of fullness like Aliyah, it's a powerful sense of presence that's tough not to notice. Presence and engagement have an impact on others and enable an individual to venture out into the world with a level of confidence and an eagerness to journey forward.

Step 3: Get to Your Core

While being fully present and engaged can take a lifetime to master, we all have the ability to focus our attention and to learn how to become more genuinely curious, connected and engaged. Otto Scharmer suggests that one way forward is to focus on the art of 'presencing'—a way of being that blends together sensing with presence, and a way of engaging that 'shifts the place of perception to the source' (Scharmer, 2007). He encourages us to open our mind, heart and will in order to let go of past preconceptions and let in new realms of thinking. To some degree, it's an argument to get down to the essentials of life, to bring our true selves to the fore and to align our values, purpose and core to our decisions and actions. In an explanation that connects to our ascending spiral model, Scharmer brings to mind the German word *Umstulpung* which translates into turning the inside out and the outside in. It's a process he explains that enables us 'to see from a different direction, you begin to move toward yourself from the future.'

Another way of understanding Scharmer's notion of presencing is to think about the illustrations shared earlier. What if there was a way to access your inner core, where you know the circle to be full of life? If we could bring forward that full and centered core, master a way to *umstulpung*, then there's nowhere for absence to reside. *Who* are we would be abundantly self-evident to ourselves and to all with whom we come in contact. We could sense more clearly and be present more abundantly. We could make presencing a regular part of our daily existence. Scharmer would say that this process of letting go of our numbness or faux facades allows us to let in our true self and facilitates our connection to others. In his model, letting go and letting in precedes our ability to co-create with others.

Beyond being present with one's self, it is the presence and connection with other human beings that can be most powerful. And much like love and other elusive concepts, it can be easier to understand 'presence' by what it's not. When you enter into a conversation, you quickly know when someone is not truly listening, not engaged, not present. Even in a classroom or at a meeting when a whole group is in attendance, it's readily apparent to a good teacher or facilitator when particular individuals are sitting in their seats but have their minds located elsewhere. Someone who is present sends off a clear signal that he or she wants to be a part of what others are doing, saying, feeling and experiencing. Someone who is not present can take up physical space but does not make any contribution to the whole.

There are often very visible detachments and barriers that people display to stay clear of being present. In a fascinating social experiment with violin maestro Joshua Bell, the musician played his instrument in the entrance of a Washington, DC, train station. He used the same 3.5 million dollar Stradivarius violin that he played in the famous New York City Carnegie Hall where people paid hundreds of dollars to listen to him. Yet, when he played the same music on the same instrument in the train station, most people ignored his virtuosity, focused on their own busy lives and remained absorbed in their own isolated existence.

Watching the passing commuters walk by the gifted musician makes the informed observer want to shout out, 'this is Joshua Bell, wake up and take notice!' It's an observation that's easy to make for those privy to the social experiment taking place, but for those in the moment and not in the know, it's an all too frequent and easy trap to fall into disconnection, disengagement and separateness. How many times a day do each of us walk by the beauty in front of us? More pointedly, what do you preoccupy yourself with as you go about each day? Maybe you're like Amie who is doing all she can to survive. Maybe you're like our friend Charlie who only listens to make sure he's giving people what they want in order to get what he wants. When your presence is only dictated by your own needs and wants, it's likely your presence isn't very strong. When your presence is rooted in trying to understand the needs and wants of others, you have at least taken a first step towards making a meaningful connection. When you avoid being curious and connected, you become a void yourself.

Lack of engagement and presence doesn't always appear so blatantly as with the case of Joshua Bell. Sadly, it's all too easy to disconnect in subtle ways as we make our way throughout the day.

We leave our home in the morning and don't really know what's on the minds of our family members. We sit in a class at school or a meeting at work and focus more on the judgements we have of others rather than simply trying to understand the essence of what people are saying. We have coffee with a friend, but fail to ask a question that really enables the person to get at something deeply troubling—something only to be shared if there's a deep connection present, a deeply connected listener. We get lazy, self-absorbed, dispassionate and absent in our lives, and we end up sucking life out of an already disconnected world rather than adding energy. There is no clear way forward when presence is absent. There's no rising within the ascending spiral when we are mired in the muck and don't clearly connect. To move forward, we must allow our core to come to the surface. We must break out of our own vicious, draining cycles and enter into more virtuous productive ones. We must engage.

There is no reason to start this journey alone. Seek out mentors, friends or even a coach, who would be willing to listen. Take notice of when you're thriving and feeling full. Consider what your own presence feels like and how you will enable others to access it.

EXPEDITION 6: SELECTING A COACH

While your individual reflection is powerful, it can be aided even more powerfully with the help of a coach by your side. A coach is someone who has your best interests in mind, can be fully present with you in conversation and is a great listener to help you process your self-exploration. Who do you have in your life who can serve in that capacity for future expeditions as you travel the ascending spiral? Who will be willing to take the time to listen to your reflections, to ask you probing questions, to respond to your own queries? Ask them now to support you, challenge you, reinforce you and often to just be your ally and friend.

To have strength for the journey ahead, use all the tools and knowledge at your disposal. Remember how others you admire move about their lives and connect. Know the story you want to tell others about yourself and what you believe in—and deeply listen to their stories. When you can be *who* you are and know your own story, you will be more curious, more engaged and more full of heart. You will be increasingly ready. And as you work towards this readiness state, there comes a time when you simply have to take the leap forward.

It's time to cross the threshold.

And begin....

WHAT'S AHEAD?

In Part II of this book, 'Crossing the Threshold', you will fully immerse as the hero of your own journey of self-discovery and explore the heights of your ability to be an effective leader that serves your organization and community. You will become clear about what it takes for you to create the positive energy of the ascending spiral for better outcomes. As you progress, you will meet many more of the leaders we have interviewed over time and provide examples of the kind of path and impact we're describing. Specifically, you will fully experience the iterative and elevating effect of examining your 'who, why, what and how' by answering the following questions:

- Who am I? What core values anchor me, drive me and motivate me?
- Why am I here? What is my life's purpose during my short time on Earth? What mission is fueled by my core values, by talents and my vision for a better future?
- What is the difference that I can make? What will be the shifted status quo that I will influence and what will be the preferred future I want to impact?
- How am I to be in the world? How will I align my skills, behaviors and dispositions in ways that will fulfill my purpose?

You'll be asked to confront your fears that have appeared in the face of naysayers, shape-shifters and adversity. You will learn to draw strength from them and then return to your family, your organization and your community with new-found clarity about your purpose, strengths, skills and attitudes. Rising through the ascending spiral can be an exciting and fulfilling journey indeed. And yet at the same time, crossing the threshold and finding your path amidst once familiar environs and into the future can be fraught with peril. And so in Part III, there will be the navigational tools provided to help prepare you for your successful return and with the ability to fully implement your new leadership capacity with skill, caring and fortitude. It's a return path in which to be successful you will need to count on all that you have amassed during your ascent through the spiral to soar in ways that feel aligned, well-grounded and transformational for yourself and those you influence.

PART II

CROSSING THE THRESHOLD

CHAPTER 4

INITIAL EXPLORATION

About Your Leap into Self-Discovery and Your Entry into Who, Why, What and How

We all have defining moments in our life—those special events or experiences that seem to mark 'before and after'. Sometimes, these are burned into our collective consciousness like when Neil Armstrong landed on the moon and we discovered that Earth was no longer our limit, or the Japanese tsunami when we faced the brutal fact that even the most advanced nation is vulnerable to the power of Mother Nature, or when Gandhi or King were assassinated and we learned once again about the worst and best of human nature. On an individual level, it may have been the moment we found true love and discovered that we could put another's needs above our own, or the loss of a parent when we realized that we had to become the grown-up, or when we found out that Santa Claus and the Tooth Fairy were mythical and we had to face the difference between fact and fantasy.

We believe that each time you cross the threshold, as Campbell calls the initiation of the hero's journey into self-inquiry, whether as a child or adult, some defining moment precipitates the work required to look within. Otherwise our comfort and complacency, our 'I'm fine' state of affairs, or our hectic daily life will rule the day. Our first journey into the ascending spiral most likely occurred in our childhood when we were trying to figure out what we really believed in and what we were going to be when we grew up. While these childhood musings may seem naïve and innocent by your standards today, they are worth examining as the starting place of your journey. Remember, we aren't leaving 'you' behind; you will still be yourself at the end of this journey. You'll just be clearer, stronger, more sure of yourself and your direction. So to begin, it's essential to understand your formative years and how the essence of who you are today started back then.

As you cross the threshold onto your path of self-discovery, we ask you to take a trip back in time—to your first foray across the threshold, before you were aware of the momentous nature of the questions you were asking of yourself. Unknowingly, this was your entry point in the inverted vortex many years ago, represented by a cross section of the spiral shown in Figure 4.1.

FIGURE 4.1 CROSS SECTION OF THE ASCENDING SPIRAL

Source: Nick Blair

Imagine that in the middle of this spiral you are asking yourself the most central question of all: Who am I? Followed closely, as you extend outwards, to the next most logical question: Why am I here? As you continue to get clarity and advance further from the center, you begin to wonder what you want to accomplish. And finally, armed with greater certainty, you can begin to ask the question: How will I get there? While this may seem like common sense, we have discovered that it's not common at all. Extraordinary individuals follow this sequence. Most of us just get busy with 'how'—the doing—rather than concerning ourselves with aligning our actions to our inner being.

This first cycle through the spiral will be drawn from your recollection of those early defining moments in your life when you begin to wonder…about yourself, your place in the world and those endless 'why' questions. It is divided into four sections corresponding to our four main lines of inquiry. At the end, there will be plenty of opportunity for you to reflect on your own answers as well as some imagined illustrative conversations from some of the greatest leaders of all time. So let's begin.

THE WHO

The 'who' represents your core self: who are you at your essence? What are your most sacred and unshakable beliefs? One sure way to discover them is to look back in time to the youthful you and to the time of your awakening to the core values that would start your journey to wholeness. But before you do, let's take a peek at what it sounds like for others to reveal their early stories. Let's imagine a round-table conversation where you can hear the early voices of Mahatma Gandhi (Mohandas in his youth), Dr Martin Luther King, Jr., St. Francis of Assisi, Mother Teresa and Muhammad discussing their early lives. In particular, their conversations begin with an early-remembered defining moment that caused them to wonder about who they are or want to be.

> Young Mohandas: *My family was Brahman, meaning we were of the professional caste and in our case that meant lawyers. I don't remember being told, but somehow I always knew that I was to become a lawyer like my father, who was an important minister in our region. It was just expected, ingrained in me, I guess. My mother was very religious and I was brought up primarily in the Hindu and*

Jain tradition of mutual tolerance and non-injury to living beings. I remember struggling as a young boy with decisions of right and wrong. I once tried meat, which was forbidden in our faith. I was disgusted with myself and asked forgiveness for such sacrilege. I was very shy in school and once an inspector came to test our class. I was unable to spell one of the words he gave us and my teacher gave me a signal to copy off of a classmate's paper. I just couldn't do it. The teacher was mad and after the inspector left, he made fun of me in front of my classmates. I became aware at an early age that my life was going to be a series of trial and errors to determine a true and honorable path forward and that this path was not going to be easy.

Young Martin: *I was born in Atlanta, Georgia, and my father was a minister. Originally my name was Michael King, Jr. named after my dad, Michael King, Sr. But when I was 5, our family traveled to Germany where my dad was inspired by the church reformer Martin Luther and changed both of our names. Quite the legacy to live up to, don't you think? My father was a successful minister and good provider for our family, but he was very clear that we were not to enjoy the privilege of class. He was also very clear that racism was an affront to G-d's will. I was also really close to my gentle mother and grandmother. My most painful memory was my grandmother's death when I was 12. I was out watching a parade against my parents' wishes when she died—it was hard to forgive myself for that, but life altering in the clarity it brought me about the importance of faith and family.*

Young Francis: *I was the son of a wealthy merchant family in Assisi, Italy. I really did grow up with a silver spoon—too much privilege and pampering, and I took advantage of it all, becoming a very popular playboy. I was generous all right; known for buying rounds of drinks at the local gathering place. I dropped out of school at 14, was bored with the prospect of going into my father's successful textile business and daydreamed of becoming a knight in shining armor (the middle ages equivalent of a superhero!). I'm ashamed to say that I sleepwalked through my wasted youth, self-absorbed with my own well-being, yet I was restless and yearning for something more—just didn't know what at the time. It wasn't until I nearly died as a prisoner of war held for ransom for a year at the age of 21 that I began to wake up and hear a deeper calling for my life. Thank G-d that G-d found me and then I was able to find myself.*

Young Agnes (Mother Teresa): *My father died suddenly when I was only 8. He was the world to me, a strong entrepreneur who provided for our family. I became very close to my mother as a result and learned from her strong faith and service disposition that our purpose in life is to serve those less fortunate than ourselves. I asked her why she invited the city's poorest to our home and she said, 'My child, never eat a single mouthful unless you are sharing it with others. Some of them are our relations, but all of them are our people.' I remember thinking, that's right. That's what I believe too—we are here to help others, I wanted to help like my mother did.*

Young Muhammad: *I was born in Mecca and came from a family steeped in the Abrahamic tradition that revered the one true G-d. It is said that I am of the bloodline of Ishmael, Abraham's son. My father died before my birth and my mother passed away when I was 5. My grandfather was a leader in Mecca who cared for the Kaaba—the original house of worship for the one true Allah. My grandfather was instrumental in fighting against the culture of false idols that had become prevalent in Mecca during that time. I remember long conversations with my mother and grandfather about how sad he was that so many had fallen away from the one true faith. I also remember them talking in low voices about how dangerous it was to fight against the power structure in Mecca at the time, which was backed by idolaters. My grandfather died when I was 8, so my uncle continued to raise me and taught me the merchant's trade. I must have developed an early belief in honesty and fairness in addition to a firm belief in the one true Allah because by the time I was 12, I was given the nickname 'Al-Ameen' which means honest, reliable and trustworthy. I was proud to be called that and thought my parents and grandfather would be proud as well.*

After reading the imagined musings of these luminaries about their youth, what did you notice they had in common and what did you notice were the unique distinctions? While their specific experiences varied, each experienced some type of awakening or call to what was most important—most impactful—on their formative core belief system. In each case, they began the inquiry of who they were becoming and the heart of their eventual message in life.

THE WHY

Our 'why', put simply, is our reason for existence. Unfortunately, some of us never completely find it, while others seem to be laser focused on their essential purpose. The clearer we become about our purpose and how it aligns with our values, the more focused our avocation or vocation in life will become. In the late teen years and early adulthood, the search usually begins in earnest and is often a roller coaster of trial and error, emotional upheaval and sometimes life-changing experiences.

Our round table continues...

> Young Mohandas: *I'm humbled to be in your presence in this discussion. It seems we have all lived a lifelong experiment in becoming all that we could become. To be honest, from my shyness as a child in school I became a pretty mediocre student, not particularly motivated by the standard curriculum. Even though I wanted to become a doctor, it was inevitable that I would become a lawyer, but that certainly didn't seem like my life's purpose. While I was in London studying law, I learned the most by reading all the books of the great world religions. It wasn't until I passed the bar and couldn't find a job that South Africa called. Little did I know that the treatment I received and observed as an Indian living in Apartheid-ruled Durban would quickly propel me to discover what I was meant to do with my life.*
>
> *The firm belief I had in mutual tolerance and non-injury to human beings ran right up against what I witnessed every day towards Indians, Colored and Black Africans. Where we could sit, eat, relieve ourselves, shop, work, live—all corners of life—were restricted according to some artificial distinction of better and worse. The level of debasement to human health and welfare was neither conscionable nor tolerable. After being thrown out of a*

courtroom in Durban for refusing to remove my turban, my most pivotal moment was on a train ride to Pretoria. I was asked to give up my seat, even though I was ticketed, and when I refused they threw me off the train at the next stop. It was then that I saw my future to fight the 'deep disease of colour prejudice'. I vowed that night to 'try, if possible, to root out the disease and suffer hardships in the process'.

Young Martin: *I too am humbled to be in the presence of this auspicious group and am really enjoying your stories. I, like you Mohandas, was not very inspired by my studies in high school or college. While I excelled and even skipped grades, I wasn't particularly motivated. I even fought against my father's conservative views and his desire for me to enter the seminary. I rebelled a bit with my choices of women to date and even partook in beer drinking. But I, also like you, eventually relented and fulfilled his wishes. It wasn't until the last year of seminary that I finally understood what ministry and religion had to do with me and the role I could play. It was the guidance of Morehouse College President Benjamin E. Mays who influenced my spiritual development. Mays was an outspoken advocate for racial equality and encouraged me to view Christianity as a potential force for social change. Now that really resonated with my values and general desire to make a difference. I could now begin to see the difference I could make.*

Young Agnes: *Very inspirational and, at the same time, it's reassuring to hear how very human we all are—flawed and yearning for something more meaningful. When I was a teenager, I sought meaning by joining a youth group called 'Solidity', run by a Jesuit priest who really taught me about the life and purpose of missionaries. By 17, I was called to become a nun and serve in India. It really wasn't until a few years later that I had an epiphany when I was ill and on a train from Darjeeling to Calcutta to recuperate. It was then that I heard my real call 'to leave the convent and serve the poor. Living among them. It was an order. I then knew...my purpose in life'. Whether it was my mother's voice calling me, my inner voice of core values or the voice of G-d—or perhaps all three—the clarity that I needed had arrived. 'Do not wait for leaders: do it yourself, one by one.'*

Young Francis: *I too am glad to hear about the early life struggles we have all experienced. I think I was the latest bloomer among us and the most stubborn resister of listening to what was right and true for my life. As I said before, it took a near-death experience to wake me up. Shortly after I was released from prison, I visited a church in San Damiano and while staring at the cross above the altar, I clearly heard a voice that said, 'Francis, rebuild my church.' Like you Agnes, I heard it as an absolute order and it gave me unshakable certainty about my future purpose. The Catholic Church was in disarray at the time and had become controlled by politics and greed, so there was a lot of rebuilding to do. Some felt that I was mentally ill and hearing voices, but to me the voices brought me clarity and certainty about my mission in life. If I was put here to reinvigorate the health of my faith and to serve the underserved, that was good enough for me, sinner that I was. It felt right.*

Young Muhammad: *Well, these are amazing encounters you are all recounting! Such impressive engagement with role models, experiences, your inner voices and even higher callings! I can identify in that I think I have experienced them all. While I learned about and believed in the one true Allah at an early age and held up values of honesty and integrity, it took me a long time to figure out my life path. I guess being such a successful merchant waylaid me for a while—life was good and very comfortable. I found my wife and had six children, and we were living well. But eventually Mecca's growing materialism and majority-held belief in idolatry started to really bother me. I began to hike up into a nearby hill and found some peace and quiet in a cave to fast and meditate without all the distractions of the bustling town. I began to have some indistinct visions, but on one occasion I felt this overpowering presence that instructed me to recite such words of beauty and force that I knew they must have come from Allah. This really shook me to my core and I couldn't really speak about it for years outside of my family. It was becoming clearer and clearer to me that I had a role to play in bringing my people back to faith in the one true Allah. But there sure was a rocky road ahead.*

It's clear from these famous stories that the road to clarity about your 'why' is neither direct nor without struggle. And while very few of us may hear voices from above, it's the willingness to wake up and listen to the voice of clarity from wherever it comes. As with these leaders and the ones we have interviewed, the moments of clarity arise through experience, hardship, dissonance and an open-hearted search for a purpose that feels right and fully aligned to our deepest held values.

THE WHAT

The 'what' is the impact you want to have within your realm of influence. Some people call it goals, others may just say it's a concrete idea of something you want to accomplish. As a child, you may not have thought about it in these terms, but you may have seen a concrete 'something' that you wanted to achieve.

And the round table continues…

> Mahatma: *It's interesting to look back at my younger self and think about what I wanted to accomplish. Though it was ordained by my family that I should study law and become a lawyer, I was never passionate about that profession and really put in a pretty mediocre effort. I always felt there was something bigger and more important that I was meant to accomplish, but it wasn't until I went to South Africa and felt the sting of the oppression of Apartheid first-hand that I realized what it was. I must have been asleep to the injustices in my home, India, but when I was subjugated to it myself, I knew that this was my charge and that the difference I wanted to make was an end to injustice on such a major scale. Though first, I must admit it, was just the Indian population I wanted to fight for—not really thinking that much about the fate of the colored or Black Africans under the Apartheid system.*

> Martin: *A really pivotal moment for me was the stand that Rosa Parks took in Montgomery, Alabama. It made me realize that the activism I had been thinking about and talking about could be real and powerful. That moment in time created the concrete idea for me that I was more than a preacher. I wanted to become an activist that made a real difference on the ground.*

Sister Teresa: *At an early age, I went to Calcutta and was living among the poor. This devastating experience burned into my young brain what the poor deal with every day, day in and day out. The people and their experience were made tangible and palpable to me in a way that made me know that I could never turn away. I saw ahead of me a life of devotion to their care and cause.*

Francis: *After I returned from prison, I could no longer look at my privileged life the same way again. A shift had occurred in the way I saw the world and I knew there was no going back. My family and friends were encouraging me to return to their fold, reassume the mantle of wealth that was my heritage and continue in the footsteps of my father. What I could see to achieve was very different. At one point, I'm sure they thought I was crazy because I stripped naked in a public courtyard ranting against the corruption in the church and among the wealthy. This was my way of saying I am different, my purpose is different, my calling is different now. I can see what I want to achieve and it isn't what you expect of me.*

Muhammad: *Years passed and I found that the beautiful words of what was to become the Koran were handed down to me through Allah. But what was I to do with such great wisdom? All that I could see at the time was that more people had to hear them and that became my life's work.*

Clearly, the 'what' varies for all of us. Our various passions around entrepreneurship, equality, justice, parenthood, education, health care and many other areas of endeavour are sometimes hard to discover. Most of our interviewees spent some time in trial and error in their early 20s and 30s discovering the corner of the world they were meant to impact. Though once found, they never turned back.

THE HOW

Our 'how' is the most pragmatic part of the model and describes behavior and actions to take that will help you to achieve your 'what'. As a child these actions may have not been very realistic, but probably gave you the opportunity to daydream about the future you and what you would look like and be like in pursuit of your early dreams

And the round table ends...

Mahatma (the honorific name he earned): *At first, I didn't know how to create change. I was very frustrated and angry, but then I found a book by Ruskin named* Unto the Last. *In it, he described a method of non-violent protest against injustice that seemed completely aligned to who I was becoming and to what I wanted to accomplish. Initially, I wasn't sure what that would look like but it gave me a much better sense of the how.*

Martin: *And I was very much influenced by you Mahatma. It was your successful struggle and non-violent protest in India that showed me the way in those early days of the Civil Rights Movement. I am so grateful that you became the standard of courage and commitment to stand up to the most violent counter-attacks with steadfastness and love. The Civil Rights Movement was a success in the USA because we followed your example for non-violent protest and persistence in the face of devastating odds.*

Sister Teresa: *I was never one for big movements or organizing large groups. I really believed that change happens one person at a time. My ministry became shaped by each individual interaction I had with the poor. I let my actions be driven by their needs, not by what I thought they needed. It was the relationship of one human to another, one listener to another, compassion and empathy for the other that was of most importance to me. This seemed like the right way for me to go about my work.*

Francis: *My role model was Jesus Christ. I wanted to emulate the way he went about his life and created change for others. I was able to eventually write this prayer that clarified my how.*

> *Lord, make me an instrument of your peace, that where there is hatred, I may bring love.*
> *That where there is wrong I may bring the spirit of forgiveness.*
> *That where there is discord, I may bring harmony.*
> *That where there is error, I may bring truth.*

That where there is doubt, I may bring faith.
That where there is despair, I may bring hope.
That where there are shadows, I may bring the light.
That where there are sorrows, I may bring joy.
That I may seek rather to comfort, than to be comforted.
To understand than be understood.
To love than to be loved.
For it is by self-forgetting that one finds,
It is by forgiving that one is forgiven.

Muhammad: *I knew from the beginning that I wasn't going to be able to do it alone. The idolaters were too many, so I was gravely outnumbered. I also learned from Jesus' story that disciples can be very helpful, so I went about spreading the word of the one Allah and gathering followers along the way. There is strength in numbers and vulnerability in isolation. I spent my time preaching about the one true G-d, engaging others in the leadership of the movement away from idolatry and towards an inclusive faith in one deity, and by committing to a movement that was not about me or us, but about the salvation of all humankind.*

While the round table serves as an illustration of how some of the great leaders of all time might have thought about their who, why, what and how, it is only that, an illustration. This is your journey, so now it's time for you to call your coach and take some time to interview each other using the line of inquiry we have prescribed in the next expedition. Simply tell your early story to one another. You'll be surprised at what you reveal about yourself if you bring your full presence and willingness to trust, connect and share. This is your opportunity to dig deep and discover the roots of your message. You'll also be amazed by the revelations your companion will share. Take advantage of this rare opportunity to connect to yourself in an untapped and in-depth manner and to connect to your coach in a manner that was until now unimaginable. It's up to you. Make the most of it!

EXPEDITION 7: DEFINING MOMENT

What was an early defining moment that caused you to pause and reflect on yourself and your future?

1. What was your defining moment?
2. What age were you and 'who' were you at that age? Your core values, your drive?
   a. Who had the greatest influence of your core values at the time?
   b. Were they tested in some way that gave you greater clarity about their importance?

While this may have changed throughout the years, looking back to the young and idealistic you provides an insight into what impressed you as important in your life.

As you progressed, did you begin to see a life purpose ahead of you that aligned with these early formed values? If so, what did you begin to see and how did it begin to form your 'why'?

3. Did you envision a way of being that seemed possible for you? Heroic, helpful, powerful, nurturing?
4. Were you influenced by someone you admired and wanted to emulate, or perhaps had a powerful experience that brought clarity?

Now let's turn your attention to your earliest version (that you can remember) of what you wanted to become or do when you grew up that (at least at the time) seemed to align with your early values and beliefs.

5. What impact did you begin to see as desirable in the world? Did you have specific outcomes in mind?
   a. Did you have a rationale about how these proposed outcomes fit with your beliefs and values, and your purpose?
   b. Did you have role models who literally were serving in a way that created similar impact?

And finally, the how.

6. How did you see yourself going about this avocation or vocation? Did your dreams align with your values?

Now that you have experienced an initial trip around the early stages of the spiral, it's time to jump forward to your current life. In the next four chapters, you have the opportunity to take a deep dive into the current you. This is the heart of the matter, and it really does matter, so please go about it with your full head, heart and presence. Time for the leap; hang on!

CHAPTER 5

YOUR WHO

About Your Current and Most Revealing Self-Examination

If I am what I have and I lose what I have, who then am I?

—Erich Fromm

Now that you've explored your early story, let's turn your full attention to your current state. You wrote a bit about your current condition in Chapter 2 after reading characters profiled. So what about the 'you' that is right here, right now? Surely by now you are ready for the most meaningful work yet, finding your message that will lead you to a future of coherence, effectiveness and fulfillment.

This time around, we will ask you similar questions about your who, why, what and how, but with some additional help from current leaders who have already given these questions some thought as they created internal alignment and a strong message of their own. By hearing their stories, it may help you to think a bit more deeply and candidly about yours. And once again, this is another opportunity to connect with your coach as you best see fit.

START WITH WHO

In 1978, a composer named Pete Townshend wrote the title song to an album for a rock band called the 'Who', with the title 'Who Are You?' Within the lyrics, the band repeats the query 'who are you' 10 times, because, as they say, they 'really wanna know'. Of course, 1978 was not the first time this question was asked, nor the first time people really wanted to know about their own, very unique identity. This ubiquitous question has been around as long as Homo sapiens and will persist for as long as our species survives. Since the evolutionary dawning of our self-consciousness, we have wondered, queried and ruminated about who the heck we are.

Often we take this question literally and answer with our name (I'm Gio), our work title (I'm a teacher), or our relationship to another (I'm Amie's mom or I'm Aliyah's brother). Sometimes we respond with our past (I went to school with you), our future (I'm going to be an engineer) or in relationship to what we own (I live in the big house on the corner and I drive a BMW). We do this because we suspect those asking don't really want more than that type of answer or, probably more often, because we are not prepared to disclose more than a surface response. Sometimes we keep it simple because we don't really want to take the time and do the work necessary for a deeper, more introspective response. But you have signed on for the latter by making it this far, so let's keep going.

Without venturing too far down the rabbit hole of psychological theory or philosophical discourse, we need to talk about identity as we explore a deeper, more authentic rejoinder to 'who am I'. Identity is the lifelong process of self-making and the key to the answer. It is no less than the mental model we form of ourselves to help us navigate in the world, interacting with others as we go, making decisions continuously along the way and establishing boundaries to keep ourselves safe.

Just as the journey through our model is iterative, so is the search for our identity: our who. We begin the discovery process in early childhood (as our round table demonstrated) and continue it through late adulthood, forging meaning as we go and developing clarity and depth of understanding about who we are as an individual and who we are in relationship to others. It is the logical place to start in our journey, because without understanding who we are, how can we possibly be clear about our purpose (why), our goals (what) and our actions (how). As Carol Hoare (2001) suggests, without a clear sense of identity, who we see ourselves to be as a person and as a contributor to society, we wouldn't be able to feel a sense of coherence throughout evolving time, social change and shifting role assignments. As a result, without a clear sense of 'who', not only would clarity be elusive, but alignment and coherence to our why, what and how impossible.

Take Helen Clark, for example. As a young girl growing up in the rural South Island of New Zealand on a successful sheep farm, she began her understanding of self by identification with her parents and nuclear family where the foundation of 'selfness' is most often imprinted. In fact, it was thought that one's self concept is solidly formed by age five as either positive or negative. Obviously, subsequent life events can shift such conception but the groundwork is nonetheless firmly laid. Helen was lucky to have a supportive family and a father, who, in particular, repeatedly declared to Helen that she could be 'whomever she wanted'. By adolescence, another pivotal period of identify formation, Helen was a strong, academically capable, if somewhat awkward pre-teen. Her father sent her to an elite boarding school in Auckland where she was immediately ridiculed for her 'southern farm roots' and her size and awkwardness. This period of challenge and adversity helped her to forge the core values that guided her throughout life and into becoming the first woman elected prime minister in her country. Throughout her adult life as a legislator, and then leader of her country, she honed her core values of fairness, safety and opportunity into policy that positively affected the quality of life of her 5 million fellow citizens. Her identity had become clearly defined as a strong New Zealand woman, a loving wife, devoted mother, clear in her convictions, sure of her leadership and successful in her service to her country.

As with Helen, our identities can be limited by negative attachments that we choose to hold onto but are enhanced when driven by clear values and beliefs. Helen could have chosen to be defined by the negative slurs she experienced at her boarding school, by comparisons to her more petite and privileged counterparts and by her inexperience in an entirely foreign school culture. But instead, she chose to create meaning out of those experiences and determine that what is most important is to be treated fairly, to be given opportunities to better yourself and to be allowed to live and learn in a safe environment. Our identity includes our vision of self in relation to gender, culture, role, status and is influenced throughout our lives by interactions and experiences that help us create meaning about our self and our place in the world. In Helen's case, she was able to use those cumulative factors and experiences to become clear about her who, to become comfortable in her own skin. Erik Erikson, the father of identity psychology, tells us that this is what we all want, a feeling of being at home on our own body, a sense of direction on our life and a sense of mattering to others (Erikson, 1994). When we are not successful at answering 'who am I', we feel confused in our role, causing serious second-guessing of our self-efficacy and an over-reliance on how others view us.

To sum up, as Parker Palmer noted, identity is an ever-evolving core within where our genetics, culture, loved ones, those we cared for, people who have harmed us and people we have harmed, the deeds done (good and ill) to self and others, experiences lived and choices made come together to form who we are at this moment (Palmer, 1999). In this chapter, you will have an opportunity to fully explore your current 'who'. By looking at your early identification with friends, family, gender, culture, ethnicity, faith as well as significant life experiences, your unique identity, and the platform upon which it rests, your core values will become clear. Figure 5.1 provides a graphic representation.

FIGURE 5.1 THE MULTIPLE DIMENSIONS OF IDENTITY

Source: Nick Blair

EXPEDITION 8: INFLUENCES ON YOUR IDENTITY

Take each factor of identify formation in the following text and reflect on both the explanation and example before you and complete the section relevant to your influences.

Factor	Explanation	Helen Clark Example	You
Family	Familial interactions are the first and most foundational for identity formation and can foster autonomy or dependency.	Mother and father's positive encouragement and creation of opportunities.	?
Friends/ Peers	Peers provide a reference point and friends influence attitudes, behavior and characteristics.	Negative interactions creating the need for safety and security.	?

Factor	Explanation	Helen Clark Example	You
Gender/ Sexuality	Gender refers to identification as male or female. Sexual identity is recognition of one's sexual attractions and behaviors.	Female in a male-dominated society; awkward teenage development.	?
Significant Experiences	These experiences are either positive or negative that form lasting memories and create meaning that influences identity.	Boarding school experience and early legislative experience helped hone values and translate them to policy.	?
Culture	The language, beliefs, values and norms, customs, dress, diet, roles, knowledge and skills and all other thing that people learn that make up the way of life of any society is culture.	New Zealand culture is made up of the more privileged Anglo-descendants and the less privileged indigenous Maori culture.	?
Ethnicity	Sense of belonging to a group that influences thinking, perceptions, feelings and behavior belonging to a specific heritage is ethnicity.	Helen was ethnically Anglo but was heavily influenced by the needs of the Maori and wanted to extend opportunity, safety and security to them.	?
Faith	Faith is religious heritage related to culture and ethnicity that influences moral and ethical orientation to the world.	Christian heritage influenced by the Golden Rule: Do unto others as you would have them do unto you.	?

EARLY FORMATION

Let's continue by examining your earliest memories of growing up. Who were the most influential people in your life and how did they influence who you have become today? Most of us can cite a parent and or other relative, family friend, having made a significant impact on our earliest identifications.

For Example

As an African American young girl in segregated Maryland in the 1960s, former US Ambassador Brenda Schoonover was deeply bonded to her mother and grandmother. These strong, proud women who didn't let artificial, cultural barriers impair their abilities to be supportive wives, mothers and breadwinners for their families. She also saw women who weren't afraid to peacefully protest racist limits or push civil rights boundaries. Consequently, she learned early on that she could be optimistic, fair-minded and determined as a young girl.

YOUR STORY: EARLY CHILDHOOD

As you describe your early childhood memories of significant others with whom you identified, think about how their influence in your life provided the foundation for who you are today. What values did they hold that you still emulate? What belief systems governed their life and were reflected in their actions that are evident in who you see yourself to be today?

____

____

____

____

____

____

When we become a bit older, being defined by those significant others in our early childhood becomes too limiting and we seek answers beyond the immediate realm of family and close family friends. Yet, we bring forward those foundational beliefs and values that have begun to form and begin looking for growth and coherence. We gradually begin to synthesize our early childhood identity with new cognitive skills and abilities, and developing aspirations for the future.

For Example

When Brenda reached junior high school age, the opportunity presented itself to join the first group of African American children to integrate the local school system. Her mother, grandmother and father all encouraged her to give it a chance, not only for herself but for the growth of her community as well. This extremely challenging experience, along with her earlier identification with the strong women in her life, led to the further formation of core values on the basis of standing up for what is right, staying strong in the face of adversity and caring for family first. She also began to realize that whatever she did as a future career, she wanted it to further her developing values of equality and fairness.

YOUR STORY: MIDDLE CHILDHOOD

As you think of your middle childhood and adolescence, what people made their mark on you—teachers, mentors, best friends? Were there role models that made you want to emulate them? Did you have significant life events that shaped your vision of yourself? Did you face challenges that honed your clarity about what's important to you?

____

____

____

____

____

____

Because identity is malleable and isn't fully formed and fixed in either childhood or by the end of adolescence, it continues to develop throughout adulthood as we make choices about career, religion, marriage, children and even retirement. This ongoing process of examining our life and evaluating our level of satisfaction or dissatisfaction returns us to the question of 'who am I?' Experiences become more complex, often challenges are ones of significant adversity or severe trauma and the choices we make become higher stakes.

For Example

When Brenda graduated college, she made the brave decision to apply for the inaugural Peace Corps group to be sent to the Philippines. This life-changing opportunity and the challenges that came along with it led her to a career path in the United States Department of State as a diplomat. Throughout her career, she served in many embassies across the world and ultimately as the ambassador to Togo. Her core values of standing up for the rights of others, for accepting diversity as a strength and her determination to find fair and positive outcomes had been shaped throughout her lifetime and successfully employed in her service to her country.

YOUR STORY: ADULT DEVELOPMENT

Wherever you are in your adult development, take the time to examine and evaluate the significant life events and choices that have brought you here today. What adversity have you faced that has clarified your values? What significant choices have you made that bring you satisfaction? What are the areas of your life that feel out of alignment and are keeping you up at night? The answers to these questions bring you up to date with an initial take on who you are today.

CAUTION

But, of course, the shaping of our identity is not quite as simple as looking at three different stages of your life. Your reflection needs to go deeper still and will require all of your intention and presence to do so. This deeper dive requires an examination of some of the hidden corners of your formation, some crevices that you have tried to forget, some discomfort you have tried to heal and some denial you have carefully crafted. Our sense of identity can be either thrown off course by over-reliance on the opinion of others or the harshness of misfortune, causing us to shape-shift to someone else's preferred view of us or fold under crises rather than create positive meaning, commitment and authenticity.

SHAPE-SHIFTING

The philosopher, David Hume says that all that we are is a bundle of perceptions at any given reference point (Hume, 2000). The 'self' for Hume, when perceived as something fixed through time, is an illusion. He holds that strict or fixed identity claims are simply false when talking about ourselves as persisting through time. The bundle of perceptions changes with each experience and, therefore, there is no one enduring 'self' that persists through each experience. If this is even partially the case, it explains why it is sometimes so easy to be influenced by others' views of ourselves. Or more so, our perceived interpretation of what others see in us, expect of us or desire from us. As social beings, we naturally care about what others think of us. We want and need to be accepted and to belong, but sometimes this can make us vulnerable to shape-shifting. By this, we mean shifting our 'who' to the shape of what others desire, expect and need rather than courageously sticking to who we really are.

From our character profiles, we can see that Amie is fighting this tendency to create a self that is perfect and perfectly in control. She is prone to accept the superwoman myth that says you can have it all as a young professional woman in a Western culture that demands perfect parenthood, a clear and well-organized house and happily-ever-after marriage. Her discontent is created when she attempts to shape into this persona of perfection because it only leads to failure, frustration and a futile pursuit of the unattainable.

What temptation have you fought against or are currently wrestling with to shape-shift into a 'who' that isn't really you? One of our interviewees, Howard Fuller, former superintendent of Milwaukee Public Schools, used to say, 'when the lights go out at night, I can tell if I have been true to "me" and to my values. If I fall asleep easily it's been a good day.' How do you know if it's been a good day for you? What are the temptations that have caused you to shape-shift in the past? What are you perhaps struggling with now?

____

____

____

____

____

____

The antidote to shape-shifting is, of course, awareness and a strong enough self-concept that first sees and then rebuffs the pull to shift away from your core values. Stephen Lutz is a talented community developer in remote villages in Kenya. He works for a non-profit organization with a strong Christian affiliation. As a Christian, he struggles with the hypocrisy of organized religion as it conflicts with his own core values. 'There is a part of me that is so tired of the narrowness of evangelical Christianity. The evangelical world would dismiss Gandhi. "He's a great guy but he's in hell" because he never knew Christ, they might say. That is not the way. We fear the doubting, but the richness of life is in the journey. We want to be in that journey. In the evangelical world, we have lost the critical thinking muscle. The struggle is positive. I really struggle with the leadership of the church in the West. It's basically an outwardly moral "to-do" list. I want more. I want more perspectives. I am a Sojourner's follower.' You can certainly hear Stephen's very real struggle with the tug and pull of conflicting core values. But as he says, the struggle is positive, because it is in the struggle that clarity can be found. The bottom line is that while other's perceptions are important, the most important view of yourself is the one you hold and hold onto for yourself.

CRISIS VERSUS COMMITMENT

There has been much researched and written about growth after trauma and leaps of insight after adversity. Our very human ability to forge meaning out of even the most dire of circumstances makes us unique among all the species of Earth. We are not only able to process how to avoid such calamity in the future but more importantly to construct meaning about our 'who' as a result of it. What does the way I reacted say about me? What was most important about what happened? What have I learned about my true commitments and myself? How has this helped me to clarify what is really essential for me? Were my values tested and how did I fare? Most leaders can relate to at least one such critical event in their lives that tested them and pushed them to ask tough questions of themselves. Many of the greats in our earlier round table suffered horrible hardships: Gandhi's mortification in Apartheid, Mandela's 27 years of prison, young Martin Luther King growing up in the deep racism of early 20th-century southern America. And yet, it was these very early formative hardships that honed their core values into the foundations that set their lives to greatness.

So take the time you need to think back about the significant challenges you have faced, or serious adversities you experienced and how you responded to them. What did you learn about yourself? In what way were you able to refine your core values even further? What clarity resulted?

____

____

____

____

____

____

AT THE CENTER OF YOUR WHO: YOUR CORE VALUES

While we have referenced core values throughout this book, we have not yet defined them. Simply put, core values are your most fundamental and essential beliefs that drive your decision-making and behavior. These values underlie how we relate to ourselves and to others, they guide our work and our interactions. Having given some thought to your identify and how it has been formed, having thought about the cautions that can lead us away from our core values and having invested in this journey so far, it's time to identify what are your top three core values. Not four, five or six. These are the unwavering guideposts in all that you do, the ones you would quit your job for, leave a relationship over, and be willing to risk your life to protect.[2]

1. ________________________________
2. ________________________________
3. ________________________________

THE TEST

Great job so far, but not so fast—you're not quite done yet! These three may or may not be your real and true core values. Let's put them to a couple of simple tests to see if they are or aren't. The first test is that of taking a stand. In other words, do these core values describe what you would really be willing to take a stand for, no matter how difficult and what the consequences? Ash Beckham, a feminist and activist for gay rights, retells the story of taking her niece to a 'Disney Frozen' party and standing in line for two hours to see the actors portraying Princesses Elsa and Anna. Towards the end of the two-hour wait, as they were approaching the front of the line, all the while with a very excited five-year-old niece, Ash placed the little girl on her shoulders to get a sneak peek at the Princesses. As they approached, a customer service representative said, 'Thanks, Dad, for being so patient. Do you want to put your little girl down now to meet the princesses?' In that moment, Ash had to decide what to take a stand for: her desire to stand up for her feminist principles and her right to have short hair and wear tailored clothes without being misidentified as male, or her niece's right to have a joyous birthday filled with pleasant surprises and without strife. In the end, she chose family over equality, but definitely had

[2] For a fairly exhaustive list, see http://corevalueslist.com/ to look for the words that best indicate what's at your core.

to experience the struggle within. This incident reinforced her strong belief in both core values but also helped her see which held priority in the moment.[3]

What have you struggled with that has forced you to take a stand for your core values? Have they been tested fully so that you can say with surety that these are the ones at your core?

____

____

____

____

____

____

Another test of core values is to determine if they are a 'should' or an 'is'. Sometimes when asked what's at our core, we are tempted to identify aspirational values, that is, those we think we should hold, either for cultural or faith reasons or just as a desire to 'be better'. And no one can fault us for that, right? We all strive to be better and want to have a compelling vision for ourselves and our future. But for this journey, it's important to identify those core values that are currently driving your behavior and will, in the next few chapters, align with your mission (why), goals (what) and actions (how). The final test comes in the form of an outside examination where by asking three people who have perceptions about you from different vantage points some key questions. You might select your boss, your co-worker and your supervisee at work. Or, you might ask your parent, your significant other and your child or perhaps a combination of people who know you at work and people who know you at home. The important criteria to use in deciding who to ask is that, collectively, they know you from diverse viewpoints. Once you have selected your participants, you will ask them two questions.

1. What behaviors most typify who I am when I am with you?
2. What core values do you think those behaviors reflect? In other words, what beliefs do you feel drive the way I act?

[3] For Ash's full story in her own words, see http://www.ted.com/talks/ash_beckham_when_to_take_a_stand_and_when_to_let_it_go

Once you ask these questions and analyze the results, you will be closer to discovering your currently held core values that form the foundation of your who and be fully ready to take up the next question, why.

So what are they really? Please list your best and final answer (for today) to the top three core values you hold dear and clearly exhibit to others.

1. ______________________________
2. ______________________________
3. ______________________________

We really want to know!

CHAPTER 6

YOUR WHY

About Your Clear and Compelling Mission

Now that you have identified your core values, wrestled with your identity and have some sense of who you are, you are hopefully beginning to recognize that you have the wherewithal to progress onwards and upwards in the ascending spiral. And while clarifying your 'who' no doubt provides the foundation upon which to build and realize a more fulfilling existence, there's a fundamental next step that's critical in learning how to get over yourself so that you can discover the path forward. To effectively enable your values to guide you in the most positive and constructive ways possible, it's absolutely critical to know your 'why'. Simply stated, knowing your 'why' means finding your mission in life, and once you accomplish this feat, you will have unlocked the door to self-empowerment, clear direction and focused influence.

To begin to get a sense of how important it is to articulate your 'why', think back to the profiles of Gio and Aarush. In Gio, you got to know someone who seems to understand that he has core values such as presence, respect and appreciation to ground him when he's feeling down or in need of inspiration. And yet by his own admission, Gio is 'lost at sea' and deeply concerned that he's stuck in a whirlwind he can't control or perhaps, even worse, he's being guided by inertia on a path leading to nowhere. Indeed he may be living the life of an explorer that his mother recognized while he was still in her womb, but alas unlike being the 'excellent sailor' that his name implies, Gio has no compass to serve as his guide, only a yearning to keep searching for what feels like an elusive life purpose. To progress from just being 'fine' to a feeling of being extraordinary, Gio is in need of understanding his 'why' and formulating his mission. Until that clarity is realized, unfortunately, he's a man who will likely keep feeling lost, continuing to venture out but be adrift, never quite knowing his next step.

And then there's Aarush. A charismatic and energetic young man who seems to live by (and sometimes struggle) with his values around family, creativity and innovation. He's apparently ready to burst with all of the fantastic ideas swirling around in his head, but can't yet navigate them all that well. Imagine if Aarush knew his mission in life! If he knew how to focus his beautiful dreams and pursue his quest to make the world a better place, he could perhaps start to conceive of ways to harness that active mind of his. And once he starts organizing his thoughts into a coherent whole, he might actually get his hands on the 'roadmap' that he seems to so desperately desire.

What if Aarush was to be able to say that he intended 'to create new ideas and innovations that serve and enhance the lives of all people'. And what if Gio recognized that for him it would be most important 'to listen intently, appreciate deeply and be present fully so that I in turn can nurture and care for my family and my community who I hold dear'. Would these declarations of mission help give clarity and focus to the lives of Aarush and Gio? We think so, and not only for them as individuals but also for the people and communities to which they're connected. This has been the case for the leaders interviewed in this book, for the students we have taught and the professionals we have trained. And most importantly, when you take the time to discover your 'why', the same result can be true for you.

IT'S NOT ABOUT THE COFFEE

One of the reasons why knowing your mission is so important is that it's a way of organizing and articulating your inner core values in a manner that directs your external ways of being and doing. Knowing your 'why' can feel like an epiphany, providing you with that 'aha' moment when you want to say, 'Eureka, I've got it! I know the direction I need to go!' This was the experience of Howard Behar, the man who became the well-known senior executive at Starbucks.

When Howard was still early on his business career and a man in his late 20s, he was working in a furniture store where he initially believed that his greatest ambition was to become the best salesman to ever work in the furniture business. He thought that was a clear enough goal in life until one day he was asked by his boss, 'Howard, what do you love more, people or furniture?' As he recalled in our interview, his supervisor helped him reshape his lens on life. 'When he asked that question, I guess it kind of stunned me and I took a week or so to think about it. As I thought about it, I realized it wasn't the furniture that I loved. It was the interaction with people. Furniture was just the vehicle that I was using at the time to enable that to happen.'

And so over time, with a new framework for his personal and professional outlook on life, Behar came to realize that if you regard employees and customers as precious human beings, everything else will take care of itself. In other words, if you engage employees as partners, they will astound you with their commitment and creativity. And if you think of your customers and communities as 'the people you serve', then the deep connection you create will pay countless dividends. And as he matured in his career, his mission that was first discovered at the furniture store did indeed pay extraordinary dividends at Starbucks. Behar realized early on that 'It's not about the coffee. It's all about the people.' And with that clarity of focus, rooted in clear core values around the worth of people and service, an international success story began to unfold (Behar, 2007).

TO SERVE IS TO LIVE

While some come to understand their 'why' through an epiphany, others have a more gradual but no less clear and profound path towards understanding their mission. Frances Hesselbein, the former CEO of Girl Scouts of the USA, fell into the latter category. As she explained to us, Francis grew up in a family that had service as a core value over generations. It started as early as the War of 1812, when her ancestors, seven brothers in all, stepped forward to serve in the military when US President Abraham Lincoln called for volunteers. Frances' father was also a soldier as were her husband and son. 'So, I just inherited it,' she explained. 'It wasn't anything I invented. In all my life, to serve is to live, has just been the best way to describe a life fully lived. We try to make a difference. And that means making a difference to the lives of people.'

It wasn't surprising that Francis eventually took on the lead role at Girl Scouts, where the stated mission is that 'Girl Scouting builds girls of courage, confidence, and character, who make the world a better place.' Nor was it startling when the Frances Hesselbein Leadership Institute was established in 1990 at the Peter F. Drucker Foundation for Nonprofit Management as a way to further its mission 'to strengthen and inspire the leaders of the social sector and their partners in business and government by connecting the public, private and social sectors with curated resources and relationships to serve, evolve and lead together'. Aligned to Francis' values, the organization became committed to fostering leadership grounded in:

- the passion to serve
- the discipline to listen
- the courage to question
- the spirit to include

At the Frances Hesselbein Leadership Institute, just as in generations of Frances' family, 'to serve is to live'.

Anselmo Villarreal, the president and CEO for La Casa de Esperanza, Inc. in Wisconsin,USA, is another example of a person who at an early age understood how his values integrated into his lifelong mission. At the beginning of his professional career, he took a job with the federal government of Mexico, his country of origin, so that he could be a public servant helping to improve the economy of his people. After graduating from college in his homeland, he ventured to the USA to earn his master's degree in economics. Anselmo continued to have a deep interest in economics and sought out ways to teach, research and learn about the role economics played in society, all while being deeply concerned about his fellow Hispanic community members and their struggle for equity, stability and growth.

Soon after coming to the USA and while still pursuing his passion for economics, Mr Villarreal was invited to learn about La Casa de Esperanza, a social services and community development agency, and to serve as its CEO. As he explained to us in an interview: 'I walked through the halls of La Casa, and I was immediately taken by the people inside and the programs being delivered. There was no doubt in my mind that it would be a place where I would be honored to serve as a leader.' In 2017, over 30 years after Anselmo first walked through the doors of La Casa, he still beamed with pride about the work to which he had devoted his life. He was continuing to serve, lead and grow an organization with a mission 'to provide opportunities to achieve full social and economic participation in society, with emphasis on the Hispanic population'—a mission that Anselmo surely helped shape from his own core values and, as he would quickly note, a mission deeply rooted in the values and needs of the community he served.

As if to further drive home the point that he was living a life guided by clear values and direction, when Mr Villarreal decided to return to school in 2010, he vowed not to pursue further studies unless every assignment and research project he undertook was directly related to his beloved La Casa organization. He received this assurance from his eventual faculty advisors and as a result in 2013 earned his doctorate in Leadership for the Advancement of Learning and Service from Cardinal Stritch University, in Milwaukee, Wisconsin. Dr Villarreal, as he is now called, focused his dissertation on the growing achievement gap between economically disadvantaged Hispanics and their Caucasian peers.

An accomplishment that no doubt was realized by a man who knew his mission and felt empowered to put his values to work towards a deeply meaningful goal and outcome.

LIVING IN YOUR LANE

Articulating your mission statement is like following a road towards a special destination that's uniquely your own. In fact, the steps of creating a powerful mission statement are much like the construction of a well-designed lane on a highway, where the passageways are not so narrow that they limit your mobility, nor are they so wide that they leave too much room to stray off course and become distracted or directionless. As illustrated in Figure 6.1, the lane you want gives you the boundaries to shape your course, but not the rigidity that can restrain your mobility and drive you into potholes.

FIGURE 6.1 FINDING THE RIGHT FIT

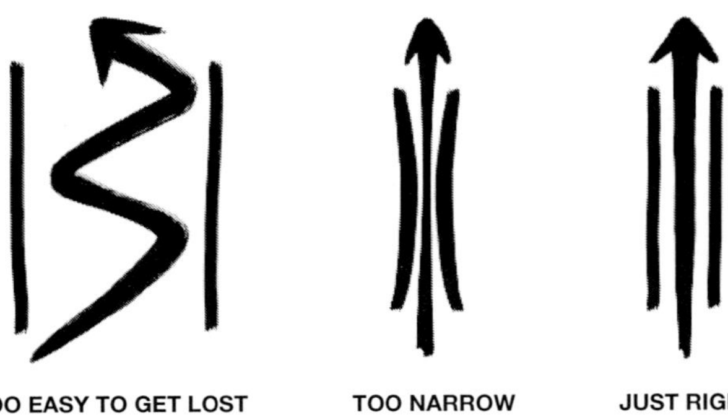

Source: Nick Blair

When you translate 'living in your lane' into how mission statements are most effectively conceived and written, consider the following three mission statements for Aliyah, our profiled CFO who held values of competency, integrity and positive influence. Aliyah is the one who said, 'Don't get caught up in a work life to impress others—rather, get caught up in an impressive life that works for you and works for others. In other words, find a path that enables you to be comfortable in your own skin and feeds the people and communities in your life that matter to you. Follow your head, heart and values—then you're more than half way home.'

> Possible mission statements for Aliyah include:
>
> Mission Statement 1: Live a life that matters.
>
> Mission Statement 2: Be a top financial leader in business who knows how to hire and develop the best people, especially women, by sharing my life of experience in ways that help businesses thrive.
>
> Mission Statement 3: Be an inspiration and source of strength for others by living with integrity, applying my successful business experience and aligning my head and heart to provide leadership that positively develops individuals, organizations and communities.

What do you notice about the possible mission statements for Aliyah? They're certainly all positive and well intentioned, but are they all effective in providing Aliyah with a well-defined path forward that's rooted in her values? Mission Statement 1, to 'Live a life that matters', is consistent with what Aliyah seems to care about, but it's so 'wide' that it doesn't help remind her of the ways in which to live her life or where she might focus her time and effort. Mission Statement 2 speaks to Aliyah's career aspirations to positively influence others, but it limits her to fulfill her mission only in her profession of financial management and primarily with women and only in the world of business. For Aliyah, this would be too constraining and not allow her to branch out in the ways she seems determined to grow. In Mission Statement 3, Aliyah appears to have found the right balance. The statement includes her values and her desire to positively impact others on the basis of her lessons learned in life and work, but it doesn't limit her from venturing out into new realms where she can realize her mission in new and fulfilling ways.

Aliyah needs a mission statement that not only serves as a helpful guide in aligning her values with actions but also one that suggests her desired impact. 'Living a life that matters' is a wonderful aspiration, but it doesn't encapsulate the sort of impact Aliyah ultimately hopes to accomplish. A strong mission statement includes values, provides clear (but not too restrictive) direction and suggests the impact you ultimately want to have. And to make a mission statement truly useful, it's important to make it a length that you can remember (one sentence is best) and a statement that uniquely represents you.

EXPEDITION 9: WRITING YOUR MISSION STATEMENT

Powerful mission statements take time to evolve. Businesses sometimes take months to articulate just the right mission statement to guide their organizations. Personal mission statements also take time to feel just right, but there's no way to land on a good mission statement without writing a first draft. In this expedition, it's time to write your mission statement for the first time or improve upon the one you already have.

Take the following steps to draft or enhance your mission statement:

1. Review the core values you wrote in Chapter 5.
2. Write down your 'assets' or the strengths that you have to offer.
3. Identify the contributions you hope to make in the world and the legacy you want your life to embody.
4. Write down three of your long-term goals in life.
5. Synthesize the components you have from completing steps 1–4 and write a mission statement that you can remember and would feel proud to share with others.
6. Share your mission statement with your coach. Ask if the mission statement you provided sounds like it's uniquely you. Do they recognize your distinctive identity in the statement and do they get a sense of your values, aspirations and impact you want to have?

This last step is about cultivating your message and gaining a sense if you are living your message out loud. If your coach and others are able to hear and identify your message and mission, then you're on the right path!

THE MANY FACES OF *WHY*

Once you start thinking and talking about your own mission, you will find it interesting to see in how many different places you meet others thinking and talking about their missions as well. You may come across people who say they are 'mission-driven' or 'on a mission', and it might be an intriguing exercise for you to see if they can clearly articulate what their mission is all about. Others won't use the word 'mission' and perhaps express themselves in terms of finding their 'calling'—a term often associated with religious leaders but now widely used by people who feel they are following a clear voice that has led them down a certain path. You may hear people describe how they were 'called' to be in a certain profession like nursing, teaching or military service. The distinction between a calling and a mission statement can be somewhat subtle, but they are not synonymous. A calling encompasses a broader and more overarching sense of direction a person feels inspired to follow. A calling does not necessarily explicitly describe a person's values, aspirations or desired impact, so usually it's not as a specific and empowering as a mission statement.

'Purpose' is another word often used in connection to a person's mission. You might have felt yourself longing to find your purpose at a point when you felt aimless or misguided. Focusing in this direction suggests a shift from the self (i.e., your who) to the other. Identifying your purpose is a helpful way of thinking about what gives your mission statement clear resolve and determination. In some ways, understanding your purpose gives you a starting point from which to launch your mission into the great beyond.

Another way you can sense that people are exploring their missions is highlighted in the title of this chapter and in the description of our ascending spiral model. Understanding and naming your 'why' can be characterized as the essential foundational step in explaining one's existence and is part and parcel of one's mission. As a way of illustrating this point, author Simon Sinek made the statement 'start with why' quite famous within business circles when he asserted that 'people don't care about what you do, they care about why you do it' (Sinek, 2011). Sinek's point was compelling because he challenged those in business to get beyond simply believing that their products or technical platforms could sustain a business, instead he pointed out how they needed to dig deeper to discover what motivated them and their customers to really believe in the product or service being offered. As catchy and compelling as 'start with why' may sound, as the model of the ascending spiral suggests, if you don't have clarity about your who, there's no foundation for your why. Or more simply put, know who or no why.

ONCE YOUR WHY IS COMPELLING, WHAT IS NEXT

Imagine if Mahatma Gandhi or Dr Martin Luther King, Jr. went through the process of Expedition 9 earlier and came to you as close friends and asked whether their mission statements were clear and distinctive. Think about your reaction as Mahatma tells you that he is driven 'to ensure with every word I utter and every action I take that I am pursuing justice through non-violence and a deep faith in humanity that results in peace and equality for all'. Consider how you would feel if Martin shared that he sought 'to fight against injustice with love that drives out hate and transforms our enemies into friends standing together and serving one another with dignity and light'. How would you react to these statements? Doesn't it seem so abundantly clear that they spoke their truth to you and that their lives were clearly guided by these missions? Further, wouldn't it be apparent that both of these men felt 'called' to live lives as servant leaders, focused on creating more just and loving societies? How will you articulate your mission so it's compelling to others and, most importantly, compelling to you?

There's another piece of the equation when exploring your 'why' that complements your mission statement and helps to complete the picture of the direction you intend your life to follow. To articulate not only the path that will guide you but also the destination you want to head, it's worthwhile to also state the vision you aspire to realize. To be able to articulate your vision, however, means you need to consider the impact you ultimately hope to realize. And to identify your impact, you'll need to move to the next level of the ascending spiral and understand your 'what'.

CHAPTER 7

YOUR WHAT

About the Direction You're Headed and the Legacy You'll Leave Behind

There was a book written by David Campbell in 1974 that was particularly memorable for its title, *If You Don't Know Where You're Going, You'll Probably End up Somewhere Else.* Even when you feel like you know who you are and the values you hold dear, and although you may have clarified a framework for your path forward, the end result of your journey won't likely amount to much if you don't have a compelling vision of where you're headed. Your 'what' is about the impact you hope to have and, eventually, it's about the legacy you would like to leave behind. Knowing your 'what' doesn't only mean seeking a destination, more importantly, it's the culmination of your actions and beliefs—delivery of the rightful message articulated by your who and why.

Our friend Chris Crowell was able to explain his 'what' many years before he ended up fulfilling his dream of building and running an eco-lodge in the middle of the Belizean rainforest. Chris was camping on his land in Punta Gorda, Belize, when he pointed out into the overgrown jungle and said, 'What would you think if I built an eco-lodge here? What if I designed cabanas that looked like they were part of the rainforest and I used local wood and materials that I would then replant and regrow? And what if I built a main lodge where guests could come together, eat food grown nearby and share stories about their adventures of the day? And what if to build and run it I employed people who live in this area and who know the land best?'

What would we think? We would think Chris was starting to speak about his vision of creating a place where he would bring neighboring communities together to welcome travellers from around the world so they could discover the wonders of gorgeous environs and a beautiful culture. He could see a place where he would put to use the lessons he learned in life, the skills and talents he had gained and the values he felt were important. You see, Chris' ideas for an eco-lodge were not hatched out of thin air or a fleeting pipe dream; they came from his early work as an art teacher who loved to create, his time outdoors landscaping the property of others, his experience managing a youth hostel that welcomed local and global travellers and from his love and respect for the people and culture of Belize.

Soon after asking 'what would you think' while camping on his land, Chris went to work on fulfilling his vision. He and his partner Jeff Pzena amassed the funds, created the business model, built strong relationships with those who lived nearby, fleshed out the design for the lodge and, step by step, they created Cotton Tree Lodge. A lodge that was eventually built with local materials (that were later replenished) by the people of the neighboring Mayan villages of San Felipe and Santa Ana. A lodge that partnered with a non-profit organization called Sustainable Harvest International to create a demonstration garden on the property that not only fed the lodge's guests but also became a place for local farmers to learn about sustainable agriculture techniques. A lodge that eventually welcomed people from all over the world and was featured on the cover of National Geographic's *Traveler* magazine for being one of the most beautiful eco-lodges in the world. While early on some might have thought Chris' vision was a flight of fancy, he knew better. Chris had conceived of his 'what' firmly rooted in the ideals and values he had nurtured for a lifetime, and that ultimately became a vision he could pursue with pride and passion.

Some people, like Chris, create visions that are particularly clear in scope around a well-defined project or program. Others, like highly esteemed leaders Sri M. N. Raju and Dr Bindeshwar Pathak, both of India, establish visions that are quite grand and transformational, with the aim of impacting large communities and societies. These are leaders who define their 'what' in bold terms and seek out multiple ways in which to shape and realize their visions.

Sri Raju, who did not have the opportunity to attend college early in his life, coupled his values of hard work and determination with his belief in the power of education to ultimately realize his vision of creating a successful group of colleges, schools and training centers. In a message on his website, Chairman Raju explains that he had a 'single-minded desire to offer a platform for youngsters to pursue basic education'. That desire resulted in his creation of the MNR Group of Institutions which started in 1974 and by 2019 was running 73 intuitions of learning ranging from play schools and high schools to degree and professional colleges. When we met Chairman Raju, we found him to be full of humility, kindness and generosity, while also being fiercely resolved to pursue his clear purpose in life. There was no doubt that he was determined to spread learning and principles of health and well-being to young people through his state of Andhra Pradesh and beyond. He had a clear sense of who he was, his purpose in life and what the destination was that he envisioned.

In many ways, Dr Bindeshwar Pathak was like Chairman Raju, humble in spirit, strong in resolve and grand in vision. However, Dr Bindeshwar, a sociologist and champion of diversity, had a very different vision that he pursued. Inspired by Gandhi's message, the good doctor committed himself to the work of restoring the human rights and dignity of untouchables, bringing them into the mainstream of society. He had a vision of giving people within the lowest caste of India a meaningful way out of their work as 'scavengers'—a way of life in which they survived by cleaning and transporting the excreta of other humans. As a path towards realizing his vision, he led the creation of the Sulabh International Social Service Organization, an NGO that built a 'sanitation movement' responsible for designing and constructing over 50 million toilets, bringing health and wellness to thousands of communities and making hundreds of towns free from scavenging. Dr Bindeshwar founded Sulabh in 1970, perhaps not initially realizing the full extent of the impact his 'what' would eventually have. Although when he led us and our group of colleagues on a tour of Sulabh in 2017 (including through his memorable World Museum of Toilets), it seemed that the doctor knew all along that his vision of a more humane approach to sanitation would help free over a million scavengers. Dr Bindeshwar, a humanist to his core, had aligned his values of equality and social justice to realize a 'what' that resulted in a huge societal shift.

We met Chairman Raju and Dr Bindeshwar fairly late in their careers when they had already been at work fulfilling their visions for over 50 years. Along with eco-lodge builder Chris Crowell, we have described those whose visions had been realized after many years of dedication. One could admire these three men, but wonder what would they have looked and sounded like much earlier in their lives. Without the benefit of hindsight, would their visions be as clear and focused? It's with that lens in mind that it seems important to learn about someone who is in the process of shaping a vision, a person much younger, a person like Mr Jamie Elder.

Jamie grew up in the city of Milwaukee, Wisconsin, USA. Milwaukee was a place built up by German and other European immigrants, made famous by large manufacturing companies and beer breweries and where today there exists a wide variety of economic classes, races and cultures. Jamie is a Black American[4] whose father was a laborer working hard and carefully saving his money, and his grandfather was a slave—an unusually close connection to an ugly part of US history for a man like Jamie who is still in his early 30s. Jamie explained to us that he grew up narrowly escaping the fate of many of his friends who got arrested and jailed by deciding to part ways with them and join the army. After the army, Jamie became an entrepreneur, trying his hand at a couple of different businesses. He

---

[4] Jamie Elder's use of the term 'Black American' versus 'African American' during his interview was intentional and therefore used throughout the narrative in order to respect his story and perspective. As with a growing number of individuals who grew up in the United States and whose families and role models were Black rather than African, Mr Elder sees himself very clearly as a Black American and he uses the term purposefully as a source of pride about his heritage and to help frame his vision for the future.

then went to work for the Wisconsin Department of Children and Families as the Director of Urban Development, and next served as the Director of Strategic Partnerships for a national organization called Stand Together. He recently launched Forty53 Advisors, a consulting firm accelerating social impact through venture philanthropy.

In 2009, Jamie read *Creating a World without Poverty: Social Business and the Future of Capitalism* by Nobel Peace Prize winner Muhammad Yunus (2007). The book, said Jamie, 'put me on my path and taught me that you don't have to sacrifice making money while doing well for the community.' He became a believer in civic social innovation and the notion that government could function better. He came to believe that 'the government safety net should be a trampoline, not a hammock'. He became focused on giving people a ladder out of poverty and economic disparity. He also learned that along with economic opportunity, 'we must intertwine good health for the mind, body and soul'. He spent time working on trauma informed care and viewed people's wealth in terms of both economic and social assets.

When we talked with Jamie, he described how he wanted to make an impact and that he had come to realize that he could only do so in collaboration with others. He explained: 'I want to know how to break the cycle of poverty in the urban core or anywhere else that it occurs. What fuels me at the end of the day is that I know that I can't do this alone. I need to collaborate, reach out and be inspired by people who will challenge me to move forward.' Jamie is on a mission to help others achieve physical and economic security and understands he needs to work with his peers to do so. 'First, my hypothesis was that it was all about having government address the issue. Then I thought government could make people rich by helping them get jobs, but I realized that could make them rich but not wealthy. We need to create wealth because that is what's sustainable. Wealth comes from ownership, so people need to learn how to be entrepreneurs to have ownership.'

In learning about Jamie, how he grew up and what he believes in, you can see how his vision has been taking shape. He has a keen sense of how his family and mentors formed him and already articulates that he wants 'to be remembered for being an active and valuable contributor to the final integration of Black Americans into the American society through economic prosperity and ownership. I want to be remembered for a pioneer in the field of social entrepreneurship and innovation. Most importantly, I want to be remembered as someone who didn't waste my life living selfishly for myself, but sacrificing and compromising when necessary for the better of others.'

What will Jamie's legacy be in 50 years from now when he has had the chance to live out his ideals like Chairman Raju and Dr Bindeshwar? Perhaps it will be the creation or leadership of a business, organization or school that builds the capacity of Black Americans to survive and thrive. Perhaps he will hold a political office that transforms a community and bolsters the society at large. Whatever the particulars are of his journey, it seems Mr Jamie Elder knows where he is heading. And, as a result, he won't end up somewhere else.

Visions are most compelling when they are aspirational, but they do not necessarily have to be grandiose or on the high order of the people you have just read about. Consider what the visions of 'ordinary' people like our characters Gio, Aarush and Aliyah look like. For Gio, whose mission was focused on listening and caring for others, surely he would be motivated by a vision in which 'every individual feels nurtured and cared for through stronger friendships, families and communities'. And Aarush seems to long for the day when his creative entrepreneurial efforts make a difference in the lives of others and create 'a world filled with innovation that enhances the quality of life and adds more joy and gusto for people young and old'. And for Aliyah, it seems she wants to see her mission of leading and nurturing others to result in 'empowered individuals and communities who realize their full potential'.

The idea here is to ponder the outcome you would achieve if you truly realized the mission you have articulated. It's about creating a vision for your future and the future of those you hope to influence. For our old friends, Mahatma and Martin, an important aspect of their power and influence stemmed from knowing that there was a crucial result they had in mind for their lifetime of work. Gandhi's vision, for example, might be simply stated through the work of the Sarvodaya Movement which seeks to realize 'welfare for all in which every individual shall live with dignity and freedom to determine his or her fate'. Dr King's vision could be summed up in his 'I Have a Dream' speech when he said his vision was that 'All men are created equal and will not be judged by the color of their skin but by the content of their character'. Through these vision statements, you can see where these great leaders were headed with their missions. Their visions broadcast to the world that they were not on a road leading to nowhere, rather, they were striving to live lives that could result in recognizable outcomes creating new realities—ones in which people would behave and relate to one another in kinder and more enlightened ways.

Of course, Gandhi and King were exceptional human beings and thinking about their visions can be intimidating. The message that can be gleaned from their visions and all the people that you learned about in this chapter, however, is not intimidating. Their visions suggest that each of us can and should be aspirational when formulating the impact we want our missions to realize. We can each be inspiring to others and ourselves when we contemplate what the world would look like if we fulfill our missions and produce the outcomes our values and purpose were designed to yield. Remember when we asked you to consider why now is the right time for you to be on this journey and why you are the one the world has been waiting for? It's time to give yourself some credit for being able to influence yourself and others to a higher ideal. And so, it's now time to articulate your 'what'—the vision you hope to realize.

EXPEDITION 10: PICTURE HOW YOUR MISSION FRAMES YOUR VISION

One way to understand and illustrate your vision is how it fits together with your mission like a picture and its frame. Your mission is the frame that provides the parameters which focus you in the direction you want to head. Your vision is the actual picture you see in front of you. Figure 7.1, based on a concept shared with us by our colleague and friend Esther Letven, provides a model for this thinking. Figures 7.2 and 7.3 apply the model to Gandhi and Jamie Elder, and finally Figure 7.4 is for you to complete. What's your frame and picture? What's your path and destination? Once you start getting clarity on these pieces, then you will not only have a firm sense of your core values and your 'who' but you will also have established your 'why' and be ready to pinpoint your 'what' and 'how'.

FIGURE 7.1 FRAMING YOUR MISSION AND VISION

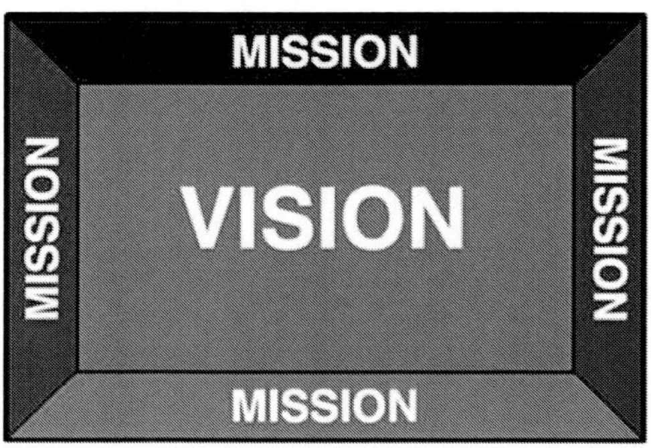

Source: The Authors

FIGURE 7.2 HOW GANDHI'S MISSION FRAMED HIS VISION

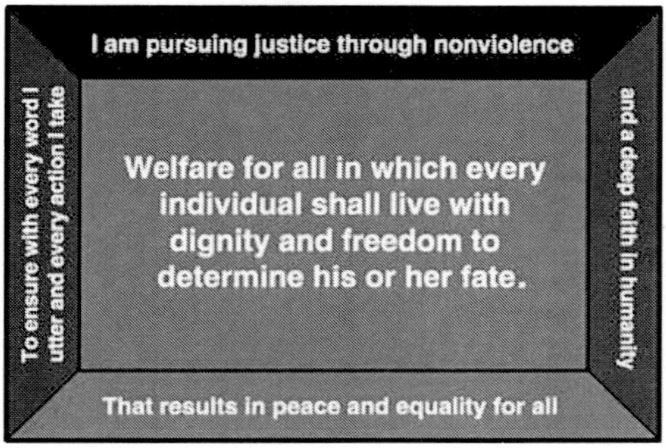

Source: The Authors

FIGURE 7.3 HOW JAMIE ELDER'S MISSION FRAMES HIS VISION

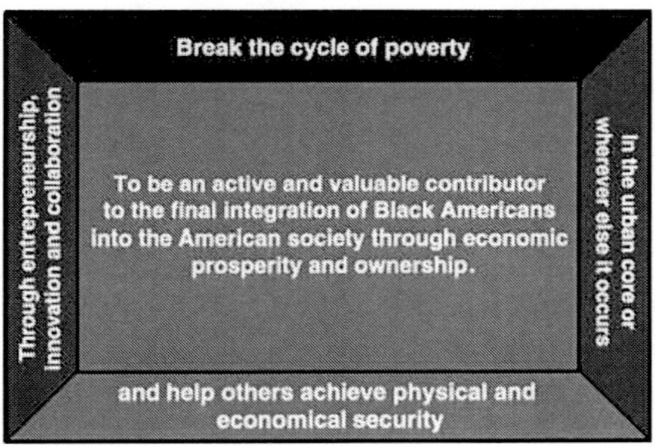

Source: The Authors

FIGURE 7.4 HOW YOUR MISSION FRAMES YOUR VISION

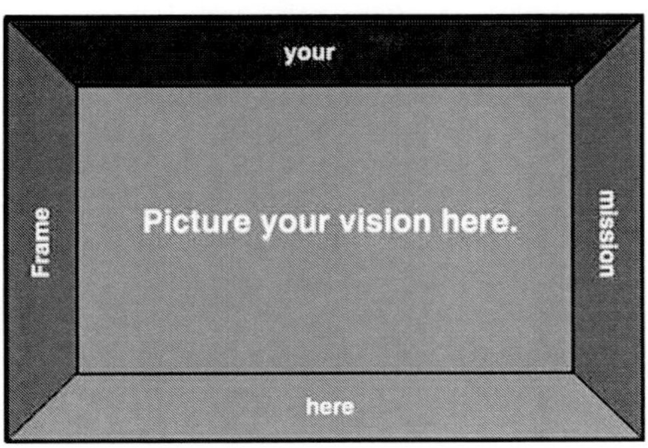

Source: The Authors

ENCOURAGEMENT ON THE WAY TO HOW

Now that you have a frame for your mission and a picture of your vision, you are likely eager and anxious to get to the all-important pragmatic next step of determining your 'how'. Getting equipped with your 'how' is actually where the rubber meets the road, where your who, why and what get 'operationalized' so that you can truly make some tangible progress forward. As you enter this next challenging point in the ascending spiral, take solace in the fact that you will not be alone. Not only will you learn about the tools and allies available to help you accomplish your 'how', but you will also find strength in the connectedness you have with others who are also striving to make a positive difference in the world. The real power of your mission and vision will be realized in connection with others who together are also working for the greater good. It is through our shared pursuit of more fulfilling, supportive and graceful lives that we will be able to collectively lift up our organizations and businesses, our communities and ourselves. It's time to let your life speak!

CHAPTER 8

YOUR HOW

About Translating Your New Alignment to Doing and Being

For the pragmatists among you, this is the long awaited 'yes, but how do you go about living, speaking and leading from your message?' It's one thing to know what you believe in, what purpose you have found for your life and what contribution you want to make, but it's an entirely different challenge to go about aligning your actions to such thoughts. This difficulty of completely integrating your who, why, what and how has plagued leaders from time immemorial and leads to ubiquitous, well-worn admonitions like:

Walk your talk
Be the change you want to see
Lead a purpose-driven life
Show me, don't tell me
Practice what you preach

These appeals are born of the struggles leaders experience with consistency, integrity and truth. Those rare leadership exemplars of alignment, like the ones in our earlier round table, stand out as shining beacons of clarity and consistency. We didn't have to worry about King reversing course, Gandhi cutting deals that compromised his values, or Mother Teresa disingenuously saying one thing and doing another. That's why we admire them. And that's also why they were so remarkably effective. If you think again of our spiral model, it makes sense that the more tightly wound the coil (as in Figure 8.1), the more powerful it becomes, not unlike a tightly coiled spring ready for a release of the energy that has been generated.

FIGURE 8.1 THE TIGHTLY WOUND ASCENDING SPIRAL

Source: Nick Blair

So now it's time to turn to the last and perhaps hardest part of your journey up through the spiral: it's time to determine your 'how'. More specifically, figuring out how you will go about aligning your actions to your values and mission. And maybe even more importantly, it's time to discern how you will be and interact in the world to shape and carry out your outlook, behavior and disposition in ways that will fundamentally shape your everyday existence.

Leading, which we have described as influence towards a desired goal, is, of course, about action; behaving in ways that are congruent with your values and purpose. Yet, leadership is perhaps even more importantly about showing up, and the way you show up means everything. This is your way of being. For example, Gandhi is most often known for his peaceful marches, strong speeches and hunger strikes to reach his goal of Hind Swaraj, Indian self-rule. But did you know that he also consistently showed up as a person of ultimate presence and compassion with those he led, even to the extent of offering tireless nursing care to a sufferer of leprosy in the Sevagram Ashram? There were not two Gandhis: the public activist and the private citizen. Rather, he was of one cloth—totally consistent and aligned in a singular tightly and powerfully wound who, why, what and how.

This, of course, will look different for each one of you depending upon your unique personal profile, but luckily, there are some well-researched guidelines that we are able to offer and are easily customizable to your distinctive who, why and what.

Jeff Blade, CEO of Matilda Jane Clothing and past executive vice president and chief financial and administrative officer at Vera Bradley, talked about experience also providing a mosaic of practice opportunities. He suggested we use 'whatever opportunity, no matter how small, to start putting your own thoughts and ideas about how it should work into practice. …It's a rich mosaic of things you thought others did well, things you vowed you'd never do yourself…. use your accumulated experiences to develop your own style.' And we would add, in alignment with your values, purpose and vision.

To this end, we are offering an easy-to-remember framework for your 'how'. It is a structure that supports your determination to take your life message and SPEAK it loud and clear with your actions and full presence. It is based on our research from interviewing hundreds of remarkable leaders around the world and additionally integrated with Martin Seligman's theoretical model of well-being. His model helps us understand the elements we can engage to create a life full of satisfaction. Each category offers a rationale for ways of doing and being that will not only increase your effectiveness, but also your overall sense of gratification and wholeness that comes from alignment to the real you (Seligman, 2012). Put simply, if your life is your message, then let your actions and ways of being SPEAK for themselves!

SPEAK: SUSTAINABILITY, PURPOSEFULNESS, ENGAGEMENT, ACCOMPLISHMENT, KINSHIP

As far back as St. Francis of Assisi in the 11th century, the notion of deed over word has been touted. St. Francis, for example, believed firmly in the words of Jesus and has been attributed as saying to his followers to 'preach the gospel at all times. Use words if necessary'. He was very aware of the emptiness of preaching and teaching when the lived example was out of alignment. More recently, Abraham Lincoln coined the phrase, 'actions speak louder than words' when speaking about the South's intentions towards the North during the American Civil War. And American humorist, Mark Twain, reminded us of how difficult the alignment of actions to words or beliefs are when he said 'actions speak louder than words but not nearly as often.'

Because a coherent 'how' is easier said than done, we offer these five propositions to guide your actions as you seek to align the way you act, show up and are perceived by others with your core values, purpose and desired outcomes in life.

- **S**ustainability: Working ourselves out of a job is always job #1 for any leader. As we devote our life to its unique purpose, our prime directive is to sustain that purpose beyond the scope of our own limitations, including our own mortality.
- **P**urposefulness: Without a laser-like focus on our unique purpose and strategic thinking about how to achieve it, the road ahead can lead anywhere, even anywhere but where we intend.
- **E**ngagement: Leadership by definition involves engagement with others in a mutually influential relationship. The minute we begin to believe that we alone are the savior is the instant we've lost credibility and the possibility of success.
- **A**ccomplishment: Again by definition, leadership has to result in some outcome. It is directional, goal-oriented and actionable.

- **K**inship: Relationships are vitally important but kinship connotes a deeper connection filled with compassion and love for the other. When ties that bind are of this nature, we have created a profound catalyst for all that we seek.

Taken together, these five guidelines create a winning combination that not only ensures powerfully coherent leadership but the pathway to a life full of meaning, satisfaction and results. Rather than a simple recipe or checklist, we offer you multiple suggestions with clear examples of how they were successfully put into place by a myriad of effective leaders.

S = Sustainability

It may seem strange to start with sustainability, but all too often it is the last or least remembered action to consider. Thinking about the long term, and particularly the term that outlasts you, is the ultimate act of optimism and possibility thinking. In our experience, effective leaders are acting from a dream (Martin Luther King), a lifelong mandate (Mahatma Gandhi) or a universal crusade (Mother Teresa). Yet, they went about their day-to-day business creating a foundation for an impact that would never be fully achieved in their singular lifetime. They were invested in both the bricks in the wall that they could place down themselves and in developing the capacity and momentum in others to finish the wall in their eventual absence. One of our friends often commented that he was concerned that the ripple effect he would leave in his wake would fade away soon after he retired. We think most of us want to spend our time investing in a better future knowing that we will leave a legacy that can be carried on, not for our own ego but for the import of the work we choose. So 'how' do we go about the work of sustainability?

By starting with the end in mind, you are purposefully integrating sustainability into the fabric of your daily existence. The ultimate goal of sustainability is to work yourself out of a job—so that others are able to fully commit and enable the work ahead without you. The following four suggestions offer you a guide to hold an optimistic outlook for the future, fill you with hope and inspire hope and capacity in others. You can accomplish this by the following:

1. *Finding opportunity in chaos, failure, crises:* Preparing for the worst and hoping for the best was the mantra of Colonel Jane Connelly stationed at a US Army hospital in Germany. She saw some real tough duty during her tenure. Some of the things she experienced could have broken the strongest soldier, but instead they renewed her hope and generosity. 'I grew up Catholic, but the experiences of going to war and places with natural disasters like Haiti and Bosnia, you see what real destitution is, what sadness is. In Bosnia, I felt this hatred and sorrow seeping my energy from the ground. Because of the genocide, I could feel the evil. It puts your own life in perspective. But now I understand that I don't need to have everything. I would love to take all the money in the world and spread it around to world for everyone to share equally.' *How do you maintain your optimism in the face of adversity?*

2. *Using humor to elevate mood in individuals and the culture as a whole:* We have a colleague, Dr Peter Jonas, who is known for his approachability because of his use of humor, particularly self-deprecating humor. Peter quips, 'I never miss a chance to laugh at myself.' Such an attitude humanizes a leader and allows for the humanity in others.

   Conversely, hubris is the enemy of leadership and the ability to make mistakes, laugh and learn from them is an important contributor to success. As former Southwest Airlines CEO Colleen Barrett so succinctly puts it: 'You know we don't take ourselves too seriously, but we take the business very seriously.' Taking ourselves less seriously allows us to move ourselves out of the way so the real work can be done. *How does your sense of humor help you keep perspective and stay positive?*

3. *Sharing leadership by working yourself out of job:* Colleen Barrett told us, 'leadership, in general, is not really a title or position, it's a way of life. I don't like the fact that many of our titles at Southwest include the word "Lead" or "Leader." Like "Station Leader" or "Lead Agent". We try to hire every person at Southwest, no matter what position they're applying for, as a leader—people who

want to motivate, people who want to be caught up in something that is far bigger than themselves. And people who want to make a positive difference. And you can be leaders no matter what level of any group or organization you are a part of.'

Colleen is a great example of a leader who works intentionally to find and cultivate the talents of others and invests in lifting up leaders all around her. Obviously, this takes an essential ingredient: humility. Leading humbly allows you to see and catalyze the magnificence of others. *How good are you at giving up control and investing in the brilliance of others?*

4. *Taking time for self-renewal and reflection, and taking care for the renewal of others:* Sustainability of self is paramount to sustainability of your mission. If you wear yourself out before your mission has been realized, you've short-circuited your ability to create a lasting legacy for the results you desire. And let's be clear, living your message is hard work. It becomes who you are in every minute of every day. And while the work is rewarding and the alignment itself is reinforcing, it's possible to become overly committed, and thus consumed. In our experience, successful leaders have an internal barometer for stress. They listen to their bodies and the chatter in their minds, finding ways to support themselves; be it exercise, meditation, walk in the woods or a glass of wine on the deck at the end of the day. Sir Michael Barber, former director of the Prime Minister's Delivery Unit under Tony Blair in Great Britain literally sought to replenish his oxygen, 'I love climbing mountains when I get the chance. That's when I clear the air.'

   And because sustainability means investment in others, you also need to monitor the wellness levels of those around you. Your compassion and love for those who share your mission result in an openness to their needs and offers you the chance to support their development and well-being as well as your own. As John Hood, former chancellor of the University of Auckland and Oxford noted in our interview, 'What is the satisfaction of leadership? For me, it is always seeing others, for whom one has an organizational responsibility, flourish and succeed as they pursue the things they want to do. That's really how I get my thrill out of this role, in seeing others do very, very well and creating the environment where they can.'

In sum, creating the future that you desire is a long-term investment requiring vision, skill, hope, inspiration, perspiration and self-awareness. By starting with the end in mind, and implementing the day-to-day actions that will lead to that end, you have effectively started working towards sustainability from the very beginning. *What are you doing today that will get you closer to the future you seek? What have you done to build the hope and capacity of others?*

P = Purposefulness

Having a purpose and meaning is not only the 'why' of our model but is essential for living a life of satisfaction and fulfillment. Beyond the pursuit of pleasure and material wealth, a greater meaning to our life gives us a reason for living that easily wins out over meager self-interest.

Indeed, the difference between surviving life and thriving in life is the awareness of your purpose. Unfortunately, many of us live without this priceless knowledge and find ourselves in boredom or apathy, with the additional distressful sense that something is missing. Without purpose, we may fill ourselves with material goods, addiction, pursuit of empty pleasures, power or fame. Conversely, when we become aware of our purpose, our why, we are awakened to a passion that catapults us forward and informs every choice we make. Our world changes. As a leader, our primary influence within an organization hangs on our ability to imbue the organization and its inhabitants with that same powerful sense of purpose. Since meaning is at the heart of our model and provides clarity around our core values and life purpose, alignment to our meaning ensures greater satisfaction and impact. You can accomplish this by the following:

1. *Clarifying your message by breaking it down to component parts, modeling it, conversing about it, presenting it and symbolizing it:*

Prasad Gollanapalli, co-founder of the Gandhi King Foundation, describes his passion for sustainable agriculture this way: 'Our role or our purpose is to talk to society and raise these questions before the people. One way to understand this is how society has gone too far in negative development. We are thinking it is positive development but as we understand and analyze it, it is negative. We have accepted whatever is happening. We have accepted chemical agriculture, but it is not necessary. We can go back to our own local seeds, local manures, local crop protection devises, local technology.' Prasad models his message by giving away toothpaste and soaps made from recycled cow manure that have proven health effects on the user. These are memorable and effective symbols of how unlikely sources can return positive and sustainable benefits. *How have you created clarity about your message for others to understand?*

2. *Over-communicating your message repeatedly, creatively, frequently:* Dick Martyr, the former executive director of American Youth Hostels, Inc. (AYH), did this in leading his national non-profit organization. Dick felt it was imperative that everyone working for AYH, and ideally all those who came in contact with it, knew the mission of the organization. It seemed in every public speech he gave, in every meeting he led and in every piece of marketing collateral he reviewed, he ensured that the mission was included. You could not work for AYH during the 1990s without knowing that its mission was 'to help all, especially the young, gain a greater understanding about the world and its people through hostelling'. It's a message that is still clearly understood by the people who run the organization today. Russ Hedge, the current President and CEO of AYH (now called Hostelling International USA) can still likely hear Dick's repeated citations of the mission resonating in his head and still likely benefits from the over-communicating Dick did to make sure the message—and the mission—got heard and understood. *What are the*

messages you need to over-communicate? How can you over-communicate in effective and creative ways?

3. *Becoming your message in all that you do, say, think, feel, be:* Tim Albright, vice president of ECHO grew up in Burkina Faso (which means land of honest men), Africa. He grew up seeing the distinct way that people lived simply and in oneness with their environment. 'What I saw demonstrated literally every day was a lifestyle and it was a mindset. It was a worldview. It was a way of interacting with one's environment and specifically in the way it tied into relationships.... my worldview has been influenced by that. It's a lifestyle. It's just the way things were. As a result, I tend to be a listener. I tend to look at things and take a little bit longer time to respond to them, perhaps more than other people, and have very few knee-jerk type responses as a result of that.'

   Gandhi famously said, 'Be the change you want to see in the world.' *In what way are you living your message for all to see? What is the 'lifestyle or worldview', as Tim says, that typifies your way of being?*

4. *Displaying authentic disappointment, outrage or creating courageous conversations when your message is jeopardized, bastardized or criticized:* When Prasad talks about Mahatma Gandhi, he describes the frustration and resulting courage that Gandhi exhibited. 'Gandhi had been a radical, because he challenged conventional notions, conventional practices, when somebody could take an advantage, or when somebody enjoyed an advantage, because of a system, whether it was Apartheid system, racial prejudice, discrimination or untouchability. So it is a process of denying something to somebody. Denying something of somebody. I have an advantage, now this selfishness that I want is something of an advantage, I will find a logic, to say why you do not deserve to get something. But in the final, large arena where all human beings are equal, this argument of denial is not tenable.' The outrage of inequality consumed Gandhi's life and fueled the powerful effect on society that he has had.

Certainly there are plenty of opportunities for modern-day leaders to voice their outrage at negative and destructive antithesis to the message they believe in. Aligned leaders take a stand against their non-negotiables—those things that are disruptive to what they value. *Are you clear about your non-negotiables? How do you take a stand for what you believe in and show appropriate outrage when the line is drawn?*

Be assured that your strength of purpose will grow as a consequence of your commitment to serve the world. With this strength, you can stay present for others and yourself in the most challenging of circumstances while continuing your work with confidence and delight.

E = Engagement

Engagement is variously defined as a promise, a pledge, an arrangement or as the act of 'being engaged'. As we use it here, we mean a commitment to be fully 'in it' not 'above it', requiring full presence, intent and interest. Those activities that require our full engagement propel learning and growth, while furthering our personal effectiveness.

We find engagement in different ways; whether it's playing an instrument, creating a work of art, reading or working on a stimulating project at work, to name a few. 'We all need something in our lives that entirely absorbs us into the present moment, creating a "flow" of blissful immersion into the task or activity.' Seligman suggests that this type of 'flow' of engagement is important to stretch our intelligence, skills and emotional capabilities. Finding flow as a leader happens when your 'who', 'why', 'what' and 'how' are fully aligned. You find the zone of peak presence and engagement. We accomplish this through the following:

1. *Getting over yourself:* A healthy ego precipitates confidence without cockiness. A healthy ego doesn't have to prove self to others because the proof is felt internally, whereas an unhealthy ego is always trying to prove worth 'out there' because there is a lack of self-worth within.

Richard Pieper, former CEO of Pieper Power, puts it this way: 'When managers, sitting on the top of corporations, or organizations or boards of directors say, "This is the idea." And 4 people or 12 people or 20 people decide, "This is the answer," they are most assuredly not on target. If you ask the people who are doing the work or the customer, "What do you think?" and you listen to that and process all that information, and it's really important, that process of going back and forth, back and forth, you will end up with something profoundly better. You'll end up with a real added value....everybody is attracted to it: employees, customers, management, everyone.'

Howard Behar went so far to create a regular reminder of how to view himself. 'I was talking about my little board of directors. So the little board of directors that sits on my shoulders is yapping at me all the time and, you know, sometimes one of them says, "Hey Howard, you're really good." Right. And I try to avoid that one. You know, they speak and I can feel good for a minute, but I realized that, for me, that's not where I want to come from. It's okay to feel good about yourself, but I need the one that says, "Okay, you're good, don't get carried away with yourself. You're just another human being doing your work."'

Keeping our egos in check is not easy but entirely necessary to fully live a life based on core principles. To truly be engaged and to engage others, a sense of humility is both required and desired. *What work do you have left to do to quiet your ego and enhance your humility?*

2. *Being clear about what is essential versus what is extraneous; avoid entanglement in the trivial:* Helen Clark, the impressive first female prime minister of New Zealand, held clear core values of fairness, opportunity and security. As a legislator and leader, her mantra was always 'If I feel that more people have opportunity to fulfill their talents, more people feel secure in New Zealand society, be they old or young and more people feeling that the government was being honest and giving them a fair go, a fair shake, than I'd be very happy.'

It seems that fulfillment and focus are also tightly aligned; the more your focus, the greater your fulfillment. *How are you learning to maximize your focus and say no to distractions? What is your 'one thing?'*

3. *Helping others identify their 'who, why and what' alignment:* Richard Pieper came to see the support of others as central to his engagement: 'At this stage, I look at the world as an organic organization, humankind. It's organic. It's all interaction. When I was younger, I would say, early 40s, not 30s, I would say that I am just a grain of sand on the beach. My job is to polish up my grain of sand. I know that every grain of sand connects with all the rest. So you polish up yours and it might have a positive effect on all the grains around you. And you've got grains of sand 360 around you.'

   Leaders tell us that the most important thing they do is hire talented people, support their talent and then get out of the way. Imagine your organization when the majority of employees were as tightly aligned as you are becoming. *Who have you invested in lately?*

4. *Consciously and determinedly staying present in the moment with a laser-like focus on your purpose:* Larry Gluth, senior vice president for Habitat for Humanity views such focus this way: 'I think for service to be truly meaningful, it does have to touch your soul. I think you do need to make that connection with those who you're serving with and those who you are in service to. And I think without that real connection, there's really so much lost. And I think we, as a society, go through the motions of so many things we do. So much of it is about your own personal satisfaction. But I think to be able to see, to find satisfaction is seeing others who are fulfilled...sometimes it's the smallest things, right? It's just a moment in time in their day that you make better. I think, sadly, so much of that seems to be far less common in today's society and the pace of everything today.'

To Larry's point, Friar Colomban, a Cistercian monk at Sénanque Abbey in Gordes, France, talked about why monks do what they do. 'But this is the lot of the monks through the centuries, to continue this liturgy and this prayer to G-d while other people are doing other things, working, keeping busy, raising children. It is our lot. It is our part in the march of the world.'

Since our purposes vary, what our presence looks like will vary as well. The important message here is that the crystal clarity that you have discovered about purpose, and the laser-like focus you have developed for accomplishing that purpose, drives your ability to be fully present—fully powerful. *What is the current opportunity for you to ramp up your ability to be fully present and fully powerful?*

5. *Engage in mindfulness practices that suit you:* Our ability to be fully present is most often cultivated by some type of mindfulness practices. Mindfulness is most often associated with meditation but it really can be any practice that works for you and builds your stamina for presence and focus. Most simply defined, mindfulness is the state of being conscious and aware. It almost seems like an oxymoron that we would need to develop a practice for such a common sense way of being. The reality is, however, that life conspires to steal our attention and cause us to worry about the past, plan for the future or perseverate on distractions rather than living in the now. Think of it this way, isn't it much better to cultivate mindfulness rather than continue to live day-to-day reacting mindlessly? Our interviewees were often engaged in such practices, among them:

   - Meditating
   - Walking in nature
   - Listening to music
   - Sitting by a window, on a porch, alone
   - Running on a beach
   - Mountain climbing

As you can see, these practices are as unique as the individuals who employ them. Engaging fully in the world makes each and every day worth living. From the moment you rise in the morning with anticipation to the moment you shut your eyes with peace and satisfaction at night, you will be living your life as few can—all in! *What mindfulness practice do you have already or might you cultivate?*

A = Accomplishment

By 'accomplishment', we mean results, the consequence, the 'what', accompanied by all the planning, trying and failing, learning and trying again that it takes to get there.

Having goals gives us a sense of accomplishment. When we achieve our goals, the sense of accomplishment motivates us to thrive by developing our self-efficacy; and the confidence and competence we need to be effective. In a nutshell, setting clear goals and achieving them builds a sense of well-being that arises from a job well done. We accomplish this by the following:

1. *Determining and setting high impact (fully aligned to core values and purpose) specific and timely goals, high leverage strategies and checkpoints along the way to measure success:* Linda Belton was a top executive in the United States Department of Veterans Affairs. She realized that unless she served the needs of employees within her organization, they would not be able to fully serve the intense and diverse needs of military veterans. She developed a program called CREW which stood for civility, respect and engagement in the workplace. These values were fully aligned with her own. Ultimately, this program served over 1,400 work groups throughout the country. As the National Director of Organizational Health for the United States Department of Veterans Affairs, she spoke to us about her most powerful strategy. 'I have one tool that I call "organizational ecology" and it's kind of a scale. I come into the office in the morning and I'll think about one side of the scale, "What do I have on my agenda today? The real-life things that I have to be worried about doing today. On the other side, on the other part of the balance are the system improvements things: "What do I need to do to strengthen and sustain my organization?" They're not

silos, separate, disparate things. It's how do I do everything that I do.'

She ends by describing as the driving force behind her clear goals and high impact strategies. 'It's part of service. It's invested employees. To me, really, everything's a ripple effect. Everything is connected.'

What goals and strategies are aligned with your values and mission and, therefore, most likely to frame and achieve the results you desire?

2. *Recognizing and acknowledging accomplishments that are mission-centric:* Linda went on to explain how everything she decides and every action she takes must be value- and mission-centered. 'Is this the day I should make this proposal or should I just back off? I take very seriously that I have to care what people think. If I let down and decide I'll practice servant leadership in the office today, but when I'm outside the office somebody catches me doing something that isn't service oriented, then that just ruined it. If I don't generate a consistent, integrated perspective, then people will call me out as a phony. And you know what, they'll be right.'

   How can you use your personal compass (your 'who' and 'why') to guide your daily decision-making in all parts of your life?

3. *Go for low-hanging fruit and high-flying ideals. One rewards; the other inspires:* Jahesh Patel is the inspirational leader of Gujarat Harijan Sevak Sangh, Safai Vidyalaya and the Environmental Sanitation Institute (ESI) in Ahmedabad, India. Through these multiple service agencies, he humbly puts Gandhi's ideals into action with immediate impact, one service at a time. His inspirational words fuel the fire of hundreds of volunteers and non-profit employees who carry out services in education, health care and sanitation for rural impoverished Indians. He talks passionately about the need to connect people to the work and each other. 'We are all one through service. The main thing is to connect people to people—connect the heart to the heart. Connecting hand, heart and head in harmony is very

important. If you work, then you understand. You put your heart into devotion and dedication into it—then you are compassionate with your thoughts. Harmony among the three is important.'

His humility is clear, 'No ambition–mission is what's important. Our work is a drop in the ocean, but a teardrop of compassion changes everything. When you serve, the universe holds you in its hands.' He goes on to make the point that everyone has a contribution to make. 'Live according to your strength. Living in the present. This is the best place for me, this is best time for me, these are the best people for me. That's living in the present. When you see the problem, your mind works. When you see the opportunity, your heart works. Be like a ladder, not like a leader. A ladder helps all to rise.' And finally, he tells us that we all must move beyond high-minded ideas and discourse. 'Love all, serve all. We can think globally but must act locally to make the immediate difference that is within each of our powers. All the ideas are there, we just have to start implementing them.'

What do you see to do immediately to put your high-minded ideals into actions that will bear fruit?

4. *Personalize the goal setting and goal accomplishment experience so that it can be fully felt by you and others:* In 1990, a team of young volunteers, inspired by Gandhian values, began gathering under the branches of a tree in the Gandhi Ashram in Ahmedabad every Saturday to play with street children. They provided the children with a nutritional meal and taught them about basic hygiene by cutting their nails and bathing them. This activity quickly came together into a full-time endeavor working to brighten the future of underprivileged children. Kiran was one of those volunteers. Today, in the Gandhi Ashram, Manav Sadhna serves more than 8,000 children and women through more than 35 projects. They also indirectly touch the lives of many more individuals through health care and educational support projects. The projects are created on the basis of the needs and participation of the community. Their

mission is 'simply to serve the underprivileged and lead with the philosophy of love all, serve all. In executing this mission, Manav Sadhna is guided by Mahatma Gandhi's unshakable beliefs in love, peace, truth, non-violence and compassion.'

The key here is community. When you try to do anything yourself, you have the power of only one. When you leverage your strength with the strengths of others, you have not only personalized your goals, but also exponentially empowered them.

All the talk in the world cannot replace accomplishment. By achieving and acknowledging results, you'll find that you and those around you not only are satisfied in the current work, but are motivated and ready to take on the work still to be done. *What are you beginning to see as the way forward for your goals, strategies and evidence of accomplishment?*

K = Kinship

Kinship is deeper than relationship. By this, we mean the ability to see the other as kin with the compassion, care, generosity, empathy, gratitude that we normally reserve for our closest and most beloved friends and relatives. Kinship means that we accept 100 percent responsibility for the success of a relationship, since it is the only portion that we can control. Kinship creates a deep connection, a bond and a sense of relatedness and affinity that goes beyond what we normally are willing to extend. Yet once created, there are no limits to what such a relationship can create!

Humans are social animals who thrive on connection, love, intimacy and a strong emotional and physical interaction with other humans. Building positive relationships with others is not only important to spread love and joy but creates greater possibility for the future. Having strong relationships gives us all support through the predictable and unpredictable challenges of life. One of the worst punishments any group of humans can proffer to another is shunning the deprivation from kinship with others. Margaret Wheatley believes that 'relationships are all there is'. Leaders are responsible for and dependent upon developing, modeling and supporting trusting relationships throughout their organizations. We accomplish this by the following:

1. *Adopting the 100 percent/0 percent approach—relationships are 100 percent my responsibility and 0 percent the other's:* Friar Columbine describes what it feels like when you have such a 100 percent investment in the other.

   'I think that what shows you whether you are in the right place or not is the feeling rooted deep down into yourself, "deep inside," that makes you experience serenity and peace, whatever happens. You remain involved in every way, every manner but nothing can pull you down really, nothing can upset you completely because of your faith and hope. Being fully invested in relationships will enable you to serve more easily, to help people in a manner not always visible but quite real.'

   This is actually a rather difficult principle to get your head around. It's so easy to think, 'but what about their responsibility—this relationship can't be all mine to cultivate'. The problem with this type of thinking is that the only person in the equation you have control over is yourself. If you give 100 percent with no expectation for any percentage in return, your chance of success increases exponentially. Who can resist 100 percent listening, 100 percent compassion, 100 percent investment coming their way? And, of course, this 100 percent must come from authentic care and concern, anything less would be disingenuous. In which of your current relationships do you see yourself giving 100 percent? *How do you envision extending this ability to others you influence?*

2. *Leading by walking around; make yourself, your real self, accessible to others:* Ruth Nyerere, the daughter of the first president of Tanzania, said about her father. 'This house was built for us by the government and he never lived in it. He didn't

want it. He lived very modestly and surrounded by people and love.' In other words, it was very important not to set himself apart from those he led. His intention was to be in constant communication with those he served and never seen as 'better than' or 'above'.

As Woody Allen, celebrated comedian and movie director, famously said, 'Eighty percent of success is showing up.' If actions speak louder than words, then your full presence shouts your intent from the rooftops. *How do you show up and remain accessible?*

3. *Connecting through curiosity—genuine care, concern, interest in and powerful listening to the other to gather perspectives beyond your own:* The greatest gift of service you can give to another person is that, for the time you are with them, they are the center of your universe.

   Executive Jeff Blade shared his deep care and concern for those in his organization. 'It's amazing in my career, how many times I've come across leaders who really don't like people. And I think if you don't like people, you just shouldn't be leading. It's literally that simple.'

   Full presence and investment in others goes beyond like to love, a word we don't often use when discussing leadership. Love can be defined as an intense feeling of deep affection. *What else might you call the driving force that makes your presence positively and fully felt by another? Do you love those you lead, serve and have a responsibility for? Even those who might annoy you from time to time?* That's the real test!

Kinship helps us build our social capital and is one of the most precious resources in any human enterprise. It means we have to get over ourselves as the holder of 'right' or 'might'. It offers us the power of partnership, connectedness and deep immersion in the needs of all.

As Meg Wheatley (2012) writes in *So Far from Home: Lost and Found in our Brave New World:*

> One of the easiest and best means for compassion to arise is in the basic human practice of talking to one another... where the rhetoric and 'isms' dissolve and we begin to relate to each other as humans just being. The more we listen, the more we recognize our common humanity, that we're all just humans sharing a common experience called life, no matter who we are or where we live. From that recognition, compassion naturally arises. It is always there, it just needs us to quiet down and become curious about one another.

In answering the questions along the way in this chapter, you have prepared yourself to integrate the elements of SPEAK into your leadership doing and being. It's time for another great conversation with your coach. This time take each of the elements of the SPEAK model and discuss how they might translate into your actions and attitude.

EXPEDITION 11: SPEAKING FOR YOURSELF

How might this look for you in your personal life, your organizational life and in your community life? As you reflect back on the five elements of SPEAK, apply them to each aspect of your life, remembering to:

- Think in a positive long-term perspective at home and at work (sustainability)

  ____

  ____

  ____

- Find the meaning in your life and what gives you a sense of purpose (purposefulness)

  ____

  ____

  ____

- Find the work that fully engages you and increases engagement in others (engagement)

____

____

____

- Set goals to achieve what's important and challenge yourself with the work you enjoy (accomplishment)

____

____

____

- Up the standard for your relationships by finding ways to deeply connect in order to understand and care about each other's perspectives (kinship)

____

____

____

Take a minute to appreciate the depth and breadth of the journey you have experienced within the pages of this book through the expeditions you have completed and the incredible conversations you have had with your coach, mentors, colleagues and friends. Very few people are as motivated as you have been to take the deep dive into self-examination and seek the opportunity for a transformation to full alignment. With this transformation comes your increased capacity to create positive change in the world by inspiring and influencing meaningful growth in others.

You are to be congratulated! You have reaped the reward, or as Joseph Campbell calls it, the 'boon' of your adventure. And, of course, you're excited to try it out, to share with others, to unveil the new you. But your journey is not quite over yet. Get ready to re-cross the threshold!

PART III

RETURNING HOME WITH INSIGHT AND RESOLVE

CHAPTER 9

RE-CROSSING THE THRESHOLD

About How to Return with Clarity, Commitment and Sustainability

The final leg of the hero's journey is the return. And, just as with your entry into the adventure, a decision must be made to re-cross the threshold to return to your family, your work and your community. As exciting as the prospect sounds, the re-entry can be filled with peril. Once you have committed to a life fully aligning your who, why, what and how, daily life conspires to pull you off track. Your family, friends and colleagues who know and love the old you may not be so enamoured with this transformed, highly aligned and purposeful new you. The old you was predictable after all: your patterns of behavior your ways of interacting with them, your way of being in the world, your own unique quirkiness. But now re-enters the new you, one who is more thoughtful, less predictable, more focused, less malleable to the manipulation of people or contexts. Be prepared for questions, temptations and perhaps even anger. Get ready for:

Why are you so intent on...
But you used to...
Come on, just do it this way for old time's sake....
I think I liked the old you better...
Who are you!

These are difficult questions to answer and will most likely take you to the edge of your comfort zone, if not into tortuous territory where you start to feel guilty for the newly aligned you. It might feel easier to relent, give in, go back, give up, but DON'T! This is your shot, your chance to drink life to the lees! And because it's so worth doing, it comes at the multiple costs of discomfort, dissonance and perhaps even the disappointment of others. Even if you find it a positive challenge to ward off such admonitions, the most severe advocate for the return to your past might be you. Habits are hard to break, mindsets are difficult to shift and maintain, and new skills and dispositions take time to cultivate. The relentless regression to the mean is a powerful force, and one not to be taken lightly. You might be tempted to wonder:

Is this really worth it?
It wasn't so bad before, was it?
Why does this have to be so hard?
What if I can't do this?

Because of this potential self-doubt, it's helpful to keep in mind that the ultimate goal of the hero's journey is to learn to live in balance and wholeness with the insight you have gained in the world you now rejoin. While such integration is difficult to achieve, and cannot occur without your focused attention and the support of others, you can bolster your readiness for this final state. We offer some guidance to first help you claim the clarity of your conviction and then intentionally seek and find the support you'll need to gain sustainable momentum forward.

And remember this caveat as well—the journey you are on doesn't end here and will no doubt continue throughout your life. Even after pursuing this quest and navigating your way through the ascending spiral, you are still fundamentally you at the core, with the same family history and cultural bearings. Your transformation lies in the increased access to and awareness of your core, and your ability to be present to it in everyday life. Now that you have more motivation and thirst to fulfill your potential, it's time to actively pursue it in ways that are wise, substantive and lasting.

COMMITMENTS AND SUSTAINABILITY

This journey was possible because it was brought to a conscious level through the expeditions offered and the hard work you engaged in to complete them. Luckily, we all have the ability to direct our thoughts, to be intentional and persistent through the extraordinary rebirthing of a new you. The transformation you have experienced is also not possible without some discomfort. In Buddhist philosophy, there's an analogy to the treatment of a wound, a physician's cleaning, probing and bandaging can cause as much pain as the wound itself—all important steps to the healing process. 'No mud, no lotus.' By learning how to accept the mud, the challenge of taking a good hard look at your life, you have discovered an unfolding ability to find the lotus, the joy of discovery and the unexpected growth to new heights.

Alas, the re-entry holds more mud to come, but best of all the possibility of more lotus as well. To help you deal with the mud, we have two suggestions for support: first, a firm and conscious commitment, and second, a well thought out plan for sustainability.

COMMITMENTS VERSUS DECISIONS

A friend of ours declared that upon his 50th birthday, he was ready for a mid-life crisis. With tongue in cheek, he described his decision to his wife, 'I can either quit my job to become a Buddhist monk or learn to fly a plane.' She, of course, while not crazy about him learning to fly, agreed that this was the preferable decision! And a big decision it was; involving expensive lessons, hours of training and the eventual hair-raising solo flight. It was on a warm, sunny morning in May that he discovered the difference between a decision and a commitment. 'When the wheels left the ground,

I realized that I, and only I, had to be fully committed to flying, so that I could return safely to the ground.'

And so it is with you. You decided to read this book. You decided to engage in the expeditions to frame your self-reflections. You could have stopped at any point in time, but you didn't. You have made it through to your own unique transformation and there is no path backward.....only forward. Now is the time for your commitment, the commitment that, once clarified, can be used as your talisman to ward off the temptations and pressures that await you upon re-entry.

While talismans are often thought of as three-dimensional objects, we suggest yours could be an empowering statement of intent and sheer will. It certainly does not sound like

I might
I could
I should

But rather it more powerfully sounds like

I will
I'm committed to
I know

For Gandhi it sounded like, 'My life is my message,' for Martin Luther King, 'I have a dream,' for Mother Teresa, 'I love until it hurts and then there is no more hurt, only love.' What does it sound like for you?

Once you have put your commitment into the words that say what you mean, you'll need a reminder to insure that you continue to mean what you say. It might be helpful to think of this talisman as the 'bumper sticker' of your life, a constant presence that brings you back to focus. Where might you place your statement of commitment in a prominent location that will serve as your reminder? Perhaps you'd like it close to that mission of yours that you created in the WHY chapter or the Mission/Vision frame you created in the WHAT chapter. Whatever you decide, claim it, proclaim it and frame it as a mantra that fuels perseverance.

SUSTAINABILITY

So now to one of the greatest challenges of your re-entry: How to sustain your clarity and commitment for the long haul. For a helpful model, we turn to the work of Ken Wilber and the Integral Institute (Wilber, 2001). Wilber has developed a map of reality that integrates different ways of knowing that humans have discovered throughout human history. He has sought to integrate knowledge from all walks of cognitive and spiritual investigation along with the ancient wisdom of the East and West into a coherent framework that finds room for the valuable contributions of all. His work is given form with four universal ways of knowing, represented by the quadrants shown in Figure 9.1.

FIGURE 9.1 THE FOUR WORLDS OF SUSTAINABILITY

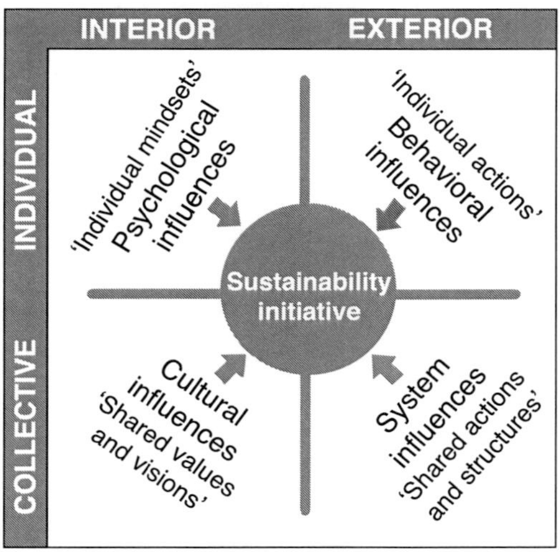

Source: Brown (2007)

Simply stated, the four quadrants can be explained by thinking about your psychological needs, your behavioral needs, your cultural/relationship needs and your structural needs to support your ongoing sustainable growth and integration over the years to come. Here's a quick summary with a few suggestions, before you dive into your final expedition and create your personal plan for sustainability.

- Psychological quadrant (upper left): This is the individual realm of your interior thought. It includes the work you have completed about your 'who' (core values) and your 'why' (your purpose in life). It also includes the mindset you carry about your ability to continue as a lifelong learner.
- Behavioral quadrant (upper right): This is realm of your individual behaviors that are observable to others and includes your 'what' (goals) that you reveal to others and well as the 'how' (actions) that they can see and respond to.
- Cultural quadrant (lower left): This is the realm of the collective culture that surrounds you. It includes the shared values and visions of your family, your workplace and your community. The degree to which these shared values are compatible or incompatible with your own can make or break your re-entry.
- Systems quadrant (lower right): This is the realm of structures that give form to your interactions in your family, workplace and community: schedules, programs and guidelines, and even unspoken rules.

For sustainability, all four quadrants should be considered. Otherwise, you invite disconnects and incoherence that will likely deliver unintended results or marginalize your impact. By creating a coherent plan for sustainability, you will be able to develop a comprehensive picture of all the dynamics at play. Such a plan offers the possibility of a clear, integrated and manageable path forward.

Just as you have experienced in the past, it will be most helpful to have conversations with your coach to help you think through your design for creating long-term balance and successful integration. Give your coach a call for this one.

EXPEDITION 12: YOUR PERSONAL PLAN FOR SUSTAINABILITY

Drawing upon the work you have done so far, and placing it in the context to which you are returning (your family, your work, your community), take some time with your coach to craft answers to the following questions. These answers will form the foundation of a comprehensive plan to re-enter successfully and sustainably!

- *Psychological:* What language will you use to communicate your clarity about your 'who' (core values) and your 'why'? These are statements that sound like with I believe or I see myself as, or what is essential for me is...Once crafted, will the same language be palatable for your various contexts? Do you need to modify the language (not the core meaning) for home or work, or your community?
- *Behavioral:* What actions will you take and in which contexts that will clearly SPEAK your intent and your values. In other words, what will walking your talk look like specifically at home, at work and in your community?
- *Cultural:* Where do you see a match between your core values and those of your family, colleagues and friends? Where do you see a disconnect or even conflict? Who will you turn to in each setting as an ally and confidant to help you make the most of the overlaps and perhaps influence the minimization of the gaps?
- *Systems:* What structures are in place that will help you achieve your goals within all three contexts (family,

work and community)? How can you best utilize these structures to create early wins for yourself and others? What structures are in place that could possibly thwart your goals? How might you partner with a like-minded ally to either change the structure or work around it, enabling you to still achieve your goals?

The journey of discovering your message and integrating it into your life represents a profound transformation from which there is no going back. As with a butterfly that breaks out of its chrysalis, you have shifted your way of being into a new way of seeing the world you influence and a way of more effectively acting within it. Where you might have been rigid, you are becoming flexible. Where you might have been closed, you are opening. Where you might have been unaware of non-productive habits, you can now see them and create a path to change them. Where you might have been attached to negative thoughts and limiting mindsets, you are learning to let go and become expansive in your outlook. And where you might have been unclear about what's most essential in your life, you are finding clarity and commitment.

Feel proud that you have devoted yourself to finding yourself no matter what the context that you came from or our returning to. You've had a grand adventure, but now it's time to return to the place where you will be for the duration. The place where no one else in this world knows better than you. It's time to put all your exploration to good use; it's time to discover home.

CHAPTER 10

DISCOVERING HOME

About Knowing Where You Belong

Now that you have traveled the path of the ascending spiral and planned for your re-entry, what have you found? At which points have you felt most alive, clear and at peace? When were you most 'comfortable in your own skin' in ways that led you to feel like you were drinking life to the lees? When were you most present and connected to the people, ideas and feelings that excite you and bring you solace? As you consider your answers, we suspect that you will also be recalling the times and places where you felt most connected to your 'who' and 'why'. You were living out your values and following your own personal mission. You were discovering home.

Home. It's an elegant concept and one with such powerful meaning that it has inspired the musings of many poets, the songs of many musicians and the prose of many writers. Perhaps part of why the notion of home is so alluring and poignant is that for a lot of people, it feels like an elusive destination. And perhaps, therein lies the paradox. So many of us seem to be searching for a place we can call home, when in fact the most extraordinary sense of home is not necessarily found in a geographic location or within a stationary structure. When it comes to describing home, there's no singular definition—no one size that fits all. That's why in this final chapter, don't expect to find a definitive description of your home because no one else but you can provide that meaning. Rather, expect to find examples and signposts that will offer you encouragement to identify your path home so that you can progress forward in your journey. Part of what you will discover too is that your 'more' resides at home, a place where you never have to settle for merely feeling just fine. Fine is okay, but it's not extraordinary, it's not home.

If the definition of home is a way of being and feeling rather than a place or destination, how do you know when you have found home? For those of you who have fully ascended the spiral and revealed your who, why, what and how, a sense of being home is clearly recognizable. And even for those who are at the early stages of the journey, discovering glimpses of home are often apparent.

Consider for a moment the characters you met at the beginning of this book, individuals who were certainly at different stages along the continuum of discovering home. Gio experienced a sense of home when he was listening intently to the stories of others or traveling to distant lands—to times and places when he felt connected to others. Amie had a sense that home, in part, when she was caring for her family. And yet, she also knew she would feel even more at home when she could find the space and time to not always feel like she was rushing through life, but instead, able to slow down and enjoy the passing of time. For Aarush, the quixotic young man with an imaginative mind and energetic spirit, home will likely be where he feels like he has started to make sense out of the chaos in his head and heart, and where he can experience life not just fully, but with purpose and direction. For Aliyah, the seasoned professional 'ready to invest' her hard-earned wisdom and personal assets into an even more deep sense of self, it seems she knew that her home could be found not in familiar, easy-to-navigate environs, but rather in places where she could be seen and understood without having to explain herself in words. And even in considering Charlie, the somewhat self-absorbed fellow who on the surface professed he only needed to know how to give other people what they wanted in order to be successful, it became apparent that he may ultimately feel more at home when he could become less concerned with acquiring things and more in tune with how to build a legacy that would make his children proud.

Along with the characters you initially met, you also have been introduced to a variety of individuals who you could certainly identify in their home environs. Imagine Anselmo Villarreal walking through his gym at La Casa and watching his children grow; picture Chris Crowell pointing to the cabanas he built at Cotton Tree Lodge, or think about Jamie Elder sensing that he just inspired the launching of a new social enterprise. Further, envision former Southwest Airlines CEO Colleen Barrett investing her time into creating future leaders, or Frances Hesselbein meeting with a group of girl scouts and inspiring them to serve their communities with courage and fortitude. It is in all of these instances when these real-life exemplars would no doubt be at home, engaged in the quest of fulfilling their missions and aligning their actions with the values they hold dear. It's an alignment that you have explored in the ascending spiral, a way of being that you have started to recognize within yourself.

Of course, it is through our luminaries that we can no doubt most easily recognize people who have devoted their lives to discovering home. You can see Dr Martin Luther King, Jr. walking home when he marched in Selma, arm in arm with other visionaries fighting for social justice and equality. St. Francis could be seen discovering home when he shed his clothing to free himself figuratively and literally to be able to serve the underserved in ways that aligned with his spirit. And surely, Mother Teresa could be found at home when she was living among the poor, addressing their needs before her own. Each of these leaders knew that being at home was only possible when they were passionately pursuing their life's work—when they were not bound up in the image of who others thought they should be, but more importantly, fully immersed in the lives they felt called to lead.

Gandhi, it could be said, invited others to visit with him at home every time he made a speech, wrote a letter, led a march, talked with world leaders and advocated welfare for all. In all of these instances, Gandhi was committed to being transparent, to let his life speak about his values and beliefs, to let others in and see who he was and where his foundations lay. In his book titled *The Unarmed Prophet*, social activist Sachchidanand Sinha paints a picture of Gandhi being most at home when he was striving to benefit others. 'Every decent person would recognize service to suffering people as a noble duty.... But with Gandhi, to serve was an inner urge whose fulfillment gave him greatest happiness.' (Sinha, 1988; p. 58). Sinha goes on to describe Gandhi's devotion to ahimsa, to reduce himself to zero in an effort to put others first and truly serve. Gandhi had the rare capacity to be at home everywhere he ventured and in every interaction.

FINAL EXPEDITION: WHERE I BELONG

Gandhi and all the other exemplars and luminaries you have met in this book found not only their 'who' and 'why' along their journeys but they all seemed to have a clear sense of where they belonged. When you understand where you belong, you feel at peace knowing you're in the right place and doing the right things that enable you and others to feel fulfilled and respected. When you feel like you belong, you feel at home. Towards that end, in this last expedition, create a list of when and where you feel like you belong. Keep adding to the list over time, noting how you feel, where you are and who you're with when you feel like you belong. It will be within this list that you will recognize your home—where you feel strong, safe, inspired, peaceful and true to your core.

The point of this last expedition is to understand the conditions that support your internal home that lives within your core. Only you know the roadmap and signposts along the way to discovering home. Creating the list of when and where you belong can help you understand your internal GPS and allow you, like Gandhi, to have the capability to be at home any place in the world. In other words, your core becomes your compass so that you'll never be lost...and always be at home.

Finding home is what's inside, not what's outside. It's not about place, although your sense of place can certainly provide an environment and more fertile grounds to feel at home. In the long run, recognizing and feeling at home is about the ongoing, internal search for who and why, and it's something that takes at least a lifetime to discover. Finding home requires discipline and paying close attention all the time. So when you get befuddled, despondent, hopeless, concerned, angry, apathetic, lazy or listless, you can snap yourself back to yourself. Back to home. Your discovery of home doesn't happen when you compare yourself to others. Your home doesn't look like anyone else's, so don't expend all of your energy attempting to be someone else's vision of who you are. You cannot, should not and will never be at home living another person's life.

If you can lead with kindness, connect with compassion and allow yourself to feel the needs of others, in all likelihood you will also become less judgemental of others and less harsh on yourself. As suggested in the last expedition, you cannot sustain a way of being or feel clearly at home when the conditions are unsettling and disturbing to you. Recognizing your comfort zone, accepting imperfections and embracing compassion, all lead you to feeling at home and being more hospitable to the world around you. You become more able to welcome others into your home. Recognize what makes you homesick and what welcomes you and others into your home. Look inside your home for love. Love for the values you have cultivated, love for the mission you have created, love for whatever impact you have had, want to have and will have, love for your own growing, learning and flawed self.

Discovering home is an action statement. It's a process, not a destination. The location exists not at a street number, but at your essence. Only you know the directions to your home, but know too that you are not alone in the journey. We are all searching for home. Home is where your truth resides and where you can thrive. It's a way of being where you and others will recognize your who and why. Wherever you are, you never feel lost when you are at home. Trust the process, follow the ascending spiral and never give up.

Head towards home and relish the journey. And let your life be your message. Always.

APPENDIX: TABLE OF LEADERS INTERVIEWED

Name	Title	Organization	Location
Anselmo Villarreal	President and CEO	La Casa De Esperanza	Waukesha, Wisconsin, USA
Bindeshwar Pathak	Founder and Director	Sulabh International Social Service Organization	Delhi, India
Brenda Schoonover	Ambassador to Togo	State Department	Brussels, Belgium
Chairman M. N. Raju	Founder and Chairman	MNR Educational Trust	Hyderabad, India
Chris Crowell	Co-Founder	Cotton Tree Lodge	Punta Gorda, Belize
Colleen Barrett	Former CEO	Southwest Airlines	Dallas, Texas, USA
Colonel Jane Connelly	US ARMY Colonel	US Army	Heidelberg, Germany
Frances Hesselbein	President and CEO	Frances Hesselbein Leadership Institute	New York, New York, USA
Friar Colomban	Franciscan Friar	Abbey	Gordes, France
Helen Clark	Former Prime Minister, New Zealand	Government	Wellington, New Zealand
Howard Behar	Former CEO of Starbucks	Starbucks	Seattle, Washington, USA
Howard Fuller	School Superintendent	Milwaukee Public Schools	Milwaukee, Wisconsin, USA
Jahesh Patel	Director	ESI	Ahmedabad, India
Jamie Elder	Managing Director	Forty53 Advisors LLC	Fort Wayne, Indiana, USA
Jeff Blade	CEO	CEO of Matilda Jane Clothing and past Executive Vice President and Chief Financial and Administrative Officer at Vera Bradley	Fort Wayne, Indiana, USA

(continued)

(continued)

Name	Title	Organization	Location
Jeff Lamb	Executive Vice President of Corporate Services	Southwest Airlines	Dallas, Texas, USA
John Burkhardt	Professor and Director of the National Forum	National Forum on Higher Education for the Public Good at the University of Michigan	Ann Arbor, Michigan, USA
John Hood	Chancellor	Auckland University and Oxford University	Auckland, New Zealand, and Oxford, England
Kiren	Founder	Ahmedabad Gandhi Ashram at Sabarmati Slum School	Ahmedabad, India
Koneru Ramakrishna Rao	Chancellor	GITAM University	Visakhapatnam, India
Larry Gluth	Senior Vice President	Habitat for Humanity, USA and Canada	Americus, Georgia
Linda Belton	Director of Organizational Health	Veterans Health Administration Centre for Organization Development	Washington, District of Columbia, USA
Paul Durante	Director	Habitat for Humanity	Pretoria, South Africa
Prasad Gollanapalli	Managing Trustee	Gandhi King Foundation	Hyderabad, India
Sir Michael Barber	Director of the Prime Minister's Delivery Unit	British Government, Office of the Prime Minister	London, England
Stephan Lutz	Director	Director, World Renew—advises local established church partners throughout Kenya, managing service program/project grants	Nairobi, Kenya
Tim Albright	Chief Operations Officer	ECHO	North Fort Myers, Florida, USA

Name	Title	Organization	Location
Richard Pieper	CEO	PPC Partners, Inc. Former CEO of Pieper Electric	Milwaukee, Wisconsin, USA
Rich Teerlink	Former CEO of Harley Davidson	Harley Davidson	Milwaukee, Wisconsin, USA
Ruth Nyerere	Teacher	Daughter of Julius Nyerere, Founding President of Tanzanian Republic	Butiama, Tanzania

Note: Titles reflect positions held by leaders referenced when interviewed for this book.

REFERENCES

Behar, H. (2007). *It's Not About the Coffee: Leadership Principles from a Life at Starbucks*. New York, NY: Portfolio.

Brown, B. C. (2007). *The four worlds of sustainability: Drawing upon four universal perspective to support sustainability initiatives*. Retrieved from http://nextstepintegral.org/wp-content/uploads/2011/04/Four-Worlds-of-Sustainability-Barrett-C-Brown.pdf

Campbell, D. P. (1974). *If you don't know where you're going, you'll probably end up somewhere else*. Niles, IL: Argus Communications.

Campbell, J. (2008). *The hero with a thousand faces*. Novato, CA: New World Library.

Coles, R. (1990). *The call of stories: Teaching and the moral imagination*. Boston, MA: Houghton Mifflin.

De Saint-Exupery, A. (1943). *The little prince*. San Diego, CA: Harcourt, Brace and World.

Dweck, C. (2007). *Mindset: The new psychology of success*. New York, NY: Ballantine Books.

Edelman, M. W. (1993). *The measure of our success: A letter to your children and mine*. New York, NY: Harper Perennial.

Erikson, E. (1994). *Identity and the life cycle*. New York, NY: W. W. Norton & Company.

Hoare, C. (2001). *Erikson on development in adulthood: New insights from unpublished papers*. Oxford: Oxford University Press.

Hume, D. (2000). *A treatise of human nature*. Oxford: Oxford University Press.

Kazantzakis, N. (1952). *Zorba the Greek*. New York, NY: Simon & Schuster.

Mann, H. (1989). *The art of teaching*. Carlisle, MA: Applewood Books.

Palmer, P. (1999). *Let your life speak: Listening for the voice of vocation*. San Francisco, CA: Jossey-Bass.

Plato. (2017). *Six great dialogues*. Mineola, NY: Dover Publications.

Scharmer, C. O. (2007). *Theory U: Learning from the future as it emerges*. Cambridge, MA: SoL (The Society for Organizational Learning).

Seligman, M. (2012). *Flourish: A visionary new understanding of happiness and well-being*. New York, NY: Atria Books.

Sinek, S. (2011). *Start with why: How great leaders inspire everyone to take action*. Westminster: Portfolio.

Sinha, S. (1988). *The unarmed prophet*. Bihar: Maral Prakashan.

Tolle, E. (2008). *A new earth: Awakening your life's purpose*. Westminster: Penguin Books.

Townshend, P. (1978). *Who are you?* Van Nuys, CA: Alfred Music Publishing.

Trungpa, C. (2014). *Smile at fear: Awakening the true heart of bravery*. Boulder, CO: Shambala.

Wheatley, M. (2012). *So far from home: Lost and found in our brave new world*. Oakland, CA: Berrett-Koehler.

Wilber, K. (2001). *A theory of everything: An integral vision for business, politics, science and spirituality*. Boulder, CO: Shambala.

Yunus, M. (2007). *Creating a world without poverty: Social business and the future of capitalism*. New York, NY: Public Affairs.

ABOUT THE AUTHORS

Nancy Stanford Blair, PhD, knew she wanted to make a positive difference in people's lives from a very early age. Once she discovered teaching as the route to touching the future, she never turned back. With a career that spans five decades creating learning opportunities at the primary, secondary, college and professional levels, Nancy has always promoted the singular and collective influence of people to transform themselves and the circumstances around them. Specifically, Nancy has created multiple local, state, national and international programs that have successfully developed inspirational, transformational leaders. She is currently Professor Emerita of Doctoral Leadership Studies at Cardinal Stritch University in Milwaukee, Wisconsin, a consultant in leadership formation and sustainability, and a proud grandmother of seven future leaders. She has co-authored four books: *Connecting Leadership to the Brain, Leading with the Brain in Mind, Mindful Leadership* and *Leading Coherently: Reflections from Leaders around the World* (SAGE). She has earned her bachelor's and master's degrees from the University of Wisconsin, Madison, and her PhD from the University of Illinois. Nancy brings her message to life through creating the unbridled capacity in others to masterfully and fully serve their corner of the world.

Mark L. Gesner, PhD, was exposed to transformational leadership early in life at large family gatherings in Brooklyn, New York, where his grandmother and great aunts inspired a sense of strength and belonging among all who entered. He sought to emulate their positive influence with his colleagues and students, and learned how to be especially impactful by traveling the world where he gained a deep appreciation for diverse perspectives and finding wisdom in unexpected places. These underpinnings informed Mark's career of building partnerships and communities, advancing entrepreneurs and organizations, and working towards social and economic impact. While in higher education, he created distinctive courses and programs focused on social enterprise, intercultural competency, and mission-driven leadership. Prior to his university work, Mark was a leader for Hostelling International USA, an organization promoting cross-cultural understanding through affordable travel. He now serves as the Maureen and Douglas Cohn Executive Director of the Tampa JCCs. He holds an undergraduate degree from the State University of New York at Albany, and graduate degrees from Harvard University and Cardinal Stritch University. Mark brings his message to life by being an engaged local and global citizen who supports others in realizing their individual and collective aspirations and to discover home wherever they roam.